Help!

My Spouse Wants Out

by
Craig Hill

FAMILY FOUNDATIONS PUBLISHING
P.O. Box 320
Littleton, CO 80160

Help! My Spouse Wants Out

by
Craig Hill

FAMILY FOUNDATIONS PUBLISHING
P.O. Box 320
Littleton, CO 80160

ISBN Number: 1-881189-04-X

Family Foundations Publishing
P.O. Box 320
Littleton, Colorado 80160

Printed in the United States of America

All scripture quotations, not otherwise noted, appear in The New American Standard Bible. The following versions have also been used: *The New American Standard Bible*, The Lockman Foundation, 1960, 1962,1963, 1968, 1971, 1973, 1975; *King James Version*, Thomas Nelson, Inc., Publishers; *The Amplified Bible*, Zondervan Bible Publishers, 1965, 12th Printing, 1975.

Contents

Dedication

To the Lord Jesus Christ,
Who gave up all He had for us.

Special Thanks to

Marilyn Conrad, Stephen R. Covey, Richard and Linda Jackson, Mike and Marilyn Phillipps, Charles Ryrie, Paul Steele, Dr. Bruce Thompson, whose teaching deepened my understanding of marital relationship.

Charissa Haines for typesetting and cover design, Ernie Haines for proofreading.

Vonnie Hill, my mother, for editing.

Gerry Hudson who provided encouragement and an Australian power cord which enabled me to finish the book on deadline while ministering in Australia.

Chapter 1

Rebuilding Faulty Foundations

So your marriage partner wants out. He/she no longer wants to remain in relationship with you. This is perhaps the most painful message that can ever be communicated from one human being to another. When the person with whom you have shared the most intimate aspects of your very being, who perhaps knows you better than any other person on earth, declares that you are not acceptable and are unfit to live with, the pain of heart that ensues is for many people the most excruciating, emotional pain of their lifetime.

Many feelings almost immediately rise up including anger, hatred, betrayal, blame and injustice (how could he/she do this to me?). Mixed along with these come fear of the future, fear of loneliness, fear of lack of finances, failure, inadequacy, guilt, worthlessness, shame, hopelessness, depression, etc. For some, for whom marriage has been filled with strife, conflict, battles or abuse, there is a sad sense of relief to think that the war might be over. In almost every case, initially there is tremendous confusion, emotional turmoil, and a lack of knowing how to properly respond. At a time like this it is critical to remove your attention from yourself, your spouse, or any other person, and focus on Jesus Christ. He alone understands your situation and can help you.

> "*I will lift up my eyes to the mountains; From whence shall my help come? My help comes from the Lord, Who made heaven and earth. He will not allow your foot to slip; He who keeps you will not slumber...*" (Psalm 121:1-3).

> "*I would have despaired unless I had believed that I would see the goodness of the Lord in the land of the living. Wait for the Lord; Be strong and let your heart take courage; Yes, wait for the Lord*" (Psalm 27: 13-14).

As you come into the presence of the Lord and begin to focus on Him, there is a two-part process which, if completed, will greatly help you. The first part is to pour your heart out to God. David, the Psalmist, was a man who frequently found himself in desperate circumstances and learned to pour out the feelings of his heart to the Lord. It is important to speak out loud to the Lord the feelings you have toward God, your spouse, any other person your spouse might be involved with, and toward yourself.

Many people have great difficulty speaking out to God negative emotions such as hatred or bitterness. They don't want to admit, even before God, that they really do feel that way. Sometimes people feel angry toward God, and this must also be expressed. If you grew up being told that it is sin to be angry or to express any displeasure toward God, this may be difficult for you. Some people are afraid that God may be angry with them or punish them for such expression toward Him. Actually, God is the only One in the universe secure enough to be railed against in anger and not retaliate or become angry Himself. If you don't speak these things out to the Lord, and release them to Jesus, it is most likely that you will stuff such emotions down on the inside of yourself, hoping that they will go away. Of course, they don't really go away. You may be able to remove such feelings from your conscious mind, but in reality you are still bearing the pain yourself, deep inside. Whatever grief and sorrow you are bearing personally, Jesus is not bearing. The Bible tells us that Jesus died to bear your sorrow and grief, (Isaiah 53:4-6). By verbally pouring your heart out to the Lord, you will find that this is God's method for you to release the anger, pain, sorrow, and grief to Jesus.

Why don't you pause and take a moment to do this right now? You may pray a prayer such as the following: "*Father God, thank You that You love me. I have been deeply hurt in my marriage by (your spouse's name). He/she makes me feel so (you fill in here with your own feelings).*" Next tell the Lord how you really feel toward Him. Lastly, express to the Lord how you are feeling about yourself.

The second critical part of the process is to ask the Lord to then show you your circumstance from His perspective. Spend some time listening to Him. This will bring you great hope. There are always four players involved in every difficult circumstance: 1) God, 2) Satan and the kingdom of darkness, 3) you, and 4) other people (namely, your spouse). Satan wants you to focus upon only one of these players, your spouse. If Satan can keep you focused on your spouse, he can keep you in a state of turmoil and frustration, because you cannot control the choices and behavior of your spouse. God wants to redirect your attention back to Himself. He also wants to show you the tactics and schemes of Satan and expose to you your part in the situation. So, after you have poured your heart out to Jesus, then spend some time listening to Him. You may have to repeat this process several times a day to continually gain God's perspective on your situation.

Let's pause and take a moment to do this right now. You may ask the Lord something like the following: "*Lord God, please show me my marriage relationship from Your perspective. What is Your plan for our marriage and future?"* (Now just wait and listen to the Lord's voice).

The Battle For Your Marriage

Let's now direct our attention to the players other than your spouse. First of all, let's start by looking at your enemy, Satan and the kingdom of darkness. It is critical for you to see that your battle is not against people.

> *"Finally be strong in the Lord, and in the strength of His might. Put on the full armor of God, that you may be able to stand firm against the schemes of the devil.* ***For our struggle is not against flesh and blood,*** *but against the rulers, against the powers, against the world forces of this darkness, against the spiritual forces of wickedness in the heavenly place"* (Ephesians 6:10-12).

There are spiritual forces of wickedness who hate you and your marriage, whose nature and purpose it is to kill, steal and destroy. Your real battle is not against your spouse, but rather against these demonic forces. This battle is not won in court or in conversation with your spouse. **This battle is won in prayer.**

> *"For though we walk in the flesh, we do not war according to the flesh, for the weapons of our warfare are not of the flesh, but divinely powerful for the destruction of fortresses (pulling down of strongholds)"* (II Cor. 10:3-4).

You must continually remember that Satan is always seeking to deceive you and your spouse. In any conversations or dealings with your spouse, you must be conscious that you are not just dealing with that person, but that there is an unseen, spiritual enemy who seeks to deceive both you and your spouse so that you cannot see each other or the situation from God's perspective. Spiritual battles are won in prayer in advance, not in conversation or interaction with your spouse. A book that will greatly help you to learn how to pray to tear down the strongholds of deception in your own mind, and pray against the deceptive strongholds which the enemy would establish in your spouse is: *First Aid for a Wounded Marriage*,[1] by Marilyn Phillipps.

Let's now turn our attention to God and look at what He is doing in your situation. God loves you and your spouse. His love always causes Him to choose the highest good for all concerned. God is the author of marriage. It is His institution. Man did not make up marriage. God did. Thus God's purpose is to preserve the integrity of His image in your marriage through healing you, your spouse, and your marriage. The destruction of your marriage is definitely not a work of God, but rather is a work of the devil. God is against the works of the devil.

> *"The Son of God appeared for this purpose, that He might destroy the works of the devil"* (I John 3:8b).

Oftentimes the devil is able to work his works of destruction as a result of areas of sin, deception, and blindness in our lives. God, however, is an opportunist Who frequently uses these same circumstances to expose to us areas in our own hearts and lives where the enemy has had access or where there has been a wrong foundation allowing Satan to work. Thus, even though God is not the author of a destructive circumstance, He will often take advantage of such a situation to expose to you wrong foundations in your heart which have contributed to the success of the devil's schemes in your life and marriage. He will then help you tear down these strongholds and rebuild the character of Christ in your life.

> "*And we know that God causes all things to work together for good to those who love God, to those who are called according to His purpose. For whom He foreknew, He also predestined to become conformed to the image of His Son, that He might be the first-born among many brethren*" (Romans 8:28-29).

God's Divine Plumb Line

Let's now turn our attention to areas of our own heart and life that God may be wanting to expose through the present circumstance. Wrong foundations certainly contribute to the crumbling of structures. Actually, it is not entirely bad when a structure which has a poor foundation crumbles and comes crashing down to the ground. There is then an opportunity to expose areas of structural weakness, clear away the rubble, reestablish a strong, unshakable foundation, and then rebuild a structure which the enemy cannot destroy. This is God's purpose in your life and marriage. God uses this very word picture several times in the Bible to describe to His people, Israel, His dealings with them. Even the very city wall around Jerusalem became an object lesson to Israel of the enemy's destruction of the nation and the hearts of the people due to a wrong foundation. We then see God's restoration of the people to the land and His command to clear away the rubble and rebuild the city wall in the sight of the enemy's continued opposition. The story of this rebuilding is, of course, found in the book of Nehemiah. We find several other pictures of the destruction and rebuilding of a wall throughout the Bible.

> *"Thus He showed me, and behold the Lord was standing by a vertical wall, with a plumb line in His hand. And He said to me, 'What do you see, Amos?' And I said, 'A plumb line.' Then the Lord said, 'Behold I am about to put a plumb line in the midst of My people Israel. I will spare them no longer"* (Amos 7:7-9).

A plumb line, of course, is used to aid in the construction of a vertical wall. Without the use of a plumb line, one cannot sight with the naked eye whether the wall is vertical or not. If a wall is not vertical, then it will have no structural integrity and will be subject to collapse from even relatively minor outside forces. God is speaking here to the nation of Israel that what they have built in their lives and culture, which they think is straight, is not straight. They have used a perverted plumb line and called straight that which is in reality crooked. God now says that He is going to bring a correct plumb line and expose to them that their wall is not straight. A crooked wall, of course, must come down and be rebuilt using a pure plumb line. God's plumb line is His Word. When life or marriage is established on anything else, it will have great difficulty standing in the face of pressure.

When you discover that a false plumb line was used or you have a faulty foundation in a structure, the safest thing to do is to dismantle that structure before it falls by accident, remove the faulty foundation, and then rebuild it using a strong foundation and a true plumb line. However, this is a lot of work, and many times people prefer to ignore the cracks that belie the faulty foundation and simply press on until enough pressure comes to cause the structure to collapse, resulting in much destruction.

> *"And when anyone builds a wall, behold, they plaster it over with whitewash; so tell those who plaster it over with whitewash, that it will fall. A flooding rain will*

> *come, and you O hailstones will fall; and a violent wind will break out. Behold, when the wall has fallen, will you not be asked,* ***'Where is the plaster with which you plastered it?'*"** (Ezek. 13:10b-12).

Rebuilding a Sandy Foundation On Rock

Whenever a wall falls, God's purpose is to expose faulty foundations and plumb lines, remove rubble and rebuild a brand new strong wall out of the old materials which He has made new.

> "*In that day I will raise up the fallen tabernacle of David, and wall up its breaches; I will also raise up its ruins and rebuild it as in the days of old;*" (Amos 9:11) "*And those from among you will rebuild the ancient ruins; You will raise up the age-old foundations; And you will be called the repairer of the breach, the restorer of the streets in which to dwell*" (Isa. 58:12).

> "*Therefore thus says the Lord God, 'Behold, I am laying in Zion a stone, a tested stone, a costly cornerstone for the foundation, firmly placed. He who believes in it will not be disturbed'*" (Isa. 28:16).

When God begins to rebuild, He starts with His own very costly cornerstone, Whom Ephesians 2:20 reveals as the Lord Jesus Christ Himself. Thus, the new structure must be rebuilt upon the foundation of Jesus Christ as the chief cornerstone, using the Word of God as a true plumb line. Before you can allow God to rebuild the structure of your marriage, you must first allow God to expose in your own life faulty foundations and perverted plumb lines. God cannot heal your marriage without first healing you. Thus, your first question needs to be, "OK Lord, what do you want to expose and rebuild in me personally?" Let's first check to see if your own life is built upon rock or sand.

> "*Therefore everyone who hears these words of Mine and acts upon them, may be compared to a wise man, who built his house upon the rock. And the rain descended, and the floods came, and the winds blew, and burst against that house; and yet it did not fall, for it had been founded upon the rock. And everyone who hears these words of Mine and does not act upon them, will be like a foolish man, who built his house upon the sand, and the rain descended, and the floods came, and the winds blew, and burst against that house; and it fell, and great was its fall*" (Matt. 7:24-27).

If your spouse has now left your marriage or wants to, then in your life the rains have descended, the floods have come, and the winds are blowing against you. How is your personal house doing? Have you found the foundation of your personal life to be built upon rock or upon sand? Is your life dependent upon your marriage and the choices of your spouse, or is your life dependent upon Jesus Christ and His choices?

Many Christians, without realizing it, empower all sorts of other people to be God to them. Many have made marriage or a marriage partner the center of life rather than Jesus' being the center of life. I have met many Christians who have been believing God for the restoration of a marriage for several years. As I have visited with some of them, it has become evident that they have not taken opportunity to rebuild a heart that seeks after God so that Jesus Christ occupies first place in their life. Rather, the focus of their life and conversation has become the return of their spouse and restoration of their marriage. In most of these situations, one of the major factors why the spouse left and has not yet returned is the idolatry of the remaining spouse. The departing spouse does not want to and cannot live up to the expectations of a spouse who has put marriage or a marriage partner at the center of his/her life instead of allowing Jesus to occupy that position. If Jesus Christ is the center of your life, then Satan cannot destroy your life through destroying your marriage.

Who is Really Your God?

In reality, whomever you let determine identity and destiny for you is god to you. What I mean by identity is simply the answer to the question, "Who am I?" Destiny is the answer to the question, "Where am I going, or what is the outcome of my life?" God is really the only One in the universe Who loves you enough to be granted authority to answer these questions. However, many people, without realizing it, unwittingly grant others the authority to determine their identity or destiny, and thus build their house upon sand. The Lord taught me this principle several years ago through an experience I had while driving in my car.

I was traveling on a two-lane highway on the outskirts of Denver. As I glanced in the rear-view mirror, I saw a car approaching from behind at approximately one-and-a-half times the speed that I was driving. When this car came close, the driver began flashing his lights at me. As he did this, I felt something rise up on the inside of me. A little voice said, "Slow down. Get in his way. Hinder him. Who does he think he is flashing his lights at me? He doesn't own this road." I slowed down a little and moved a bit more over into the center of the road, just to hinder the other driver from passing.

This action forced the other car to slow down and wait for an opportunity to pass. The driver positioned his car right behind me as though he were going to push me along. I found myself full of anger and hatred toward a man I didn't even know and had never met. At this point, I began to dialogue with the Lord. I asked Him why a simple thing like another driver's wanting to pass had so angered me. The Holy Spirit spoke back to me with a very strange reply. He said, "You are so full of anger and hatred, because you haven't asked Me, THE QUESTION." I then queried, "What is THE QUESTION?" The Lord replied, "The question is, 'WHO AM I?'" He then explained to me something like the following: "When the other driver flashed his lights and came right up and sat on your bumper, he conveyed a relational message to you that he is important, and you are of no value. He sent you a message which said, 'I'm somebody. I have places to go, people to see, things to do. You are in my way. Now move, you worthless nobody!'"

"When that message hit your heart, it deeply wounded you and stirred up the shame, worthlessness, and fear which were already latent there." I argued, "But, Lord, I don't feel worthless inside." He continued, "If that were true, then the message would not have found a place of agreement in your heart, and you would not be fighting to disprove that message right now.

"Actually, the relational message wounded you, because your heart agreed with it. The hurt from this message stirred up in you the fear of being worthless, which then began to torment your soul. So your flesh went to work on a plan to make you feel better and restore peace to your soul. Your flesh told you, 'Hinder him. Get in his way. If he thinks he owns this road, show him that he does not. Since he has exalted himself above you, just exalt yourself above him. Show him that he can't control you. You will control him.' Your flesh told you that if you do this, you will feel better. It will ease the pain inside."

The Lord continued, "You never asked Me the question, 'Who am I?' That is the real issue at stake. The man in the car behind sent you a relational message about you, and you simply received it. You never even bothered to check it out with Me. Now your soul is tormented by that message, and your flesh is fighting very hard to save your own soul life. In receiving that relational message, you entered into idolatry and declared the man in the car behind you to be god. You granted him authority to tell you who you are."

The Lord then said, "Please ask Me the question." So I did. "Lord, who am I in Your sight?" As I asked this simple question, an amazing thing began to take place. God Almighty began to bless my identity. My heavenly Father said, "Son, I love you. You are precious to Me. You are worth the life of Jesus to Me. I am so proud to call you My son. Let Me wrap My arms around you and love you. You are secure in Me. No one can shake My love for you or your destiny which I have planned for you."

As the Father was speaking these things to me, I began to feel more loved than I ever had in my life before. I felt totally secure, safe, and loved. Tears began to stream down my face, and I sensed the presence of God all over me. All the feeling of anger and hatred toward the other driver completely melted away in the love of the Father. Hatred and anger are rooted in fear. At that moment, I understood as I never had before, what the Bible means when it says, "perfect love casts out fear."

The Lord then spoke again, "Now that you have asked Me THE QUESTION, please forgive the other driver." It was now easy for me to forgive the man. My heart was absolutely devoid of any anger or ill feeling toward him. It had all melted away in the love of God. I quickly forgave the other driver and moved out of the way to let him pass.

It is critical for you to check your own heart regarding idolatry toward your spouse. If you have found that your spouse has been the center of your life rather than Jesus occupying that position, you need to repent of idolatry, revoke the authority given to your spouse to determine who you are or the outcome of your life, and then grant that authority to Jesus Christ alone.

Many times circumstances appear as though another person does have authority to shape the future of our lives. But the truth is that they really do not. To believe that your marriage partner, alone, has the power to shape the future of your life or family is practical atheism. It is to deny the authority and power of God. Joseph's brothers thought that once they sold him into slavery in Egypt that they were rid of him for good, but they were not God, and God had other plans for Joseph and his brothers. Haman thought that once he was able to get the king to sign a decree granting him authority to annihilate the Jews he would be rid of Mordecai and all the Jews for good, but Haman was not God and God had other plans for Mordecai and the Jews. Daniel's enemies thought that once they were able to get the king to throw Daniel into the lions' den they were rid of Daniel forever, but these enemies were not God, and God had other plans for Daniel and his enemies. Your spouse may think that he/she can forsake his/her marriage vows, refuse to deal with real issues and abandon you, **but your spouse is not God, and God has other plans for you and your family.**

I learned another important principle in that experience with the tailgater. IT IS IMPOSSIBLE TO FORGIVE ANOTHER PERSON UNTIL YOU HAVE ASKED GOD THE IDENTITY OR DESTINY QUESTION AND RECEIVED HIS LOVE FOR YOU. The reason for this is that your identity or destiny is always an issue when forgiveness is at stake. It is impossible to forgive someone toward whom you are still in idolatry. Unforgiveness is always idolatry, because it continues to authorize another person to determine your identity or destiny, instead of granting that authority to God.

If you have ever tried to forgive someone who has deeply wounded you without revoking the authority you have granted him/her to determine your identity and destiny, you know that it is impossible to effect real forgiveness in your heart. You must go to God and ask Him THE QUESTION first. Many have tried to forgive "by faith," which is just a choice of the will. But it never releases the heart.

By going to God and asking Him to answer these key questions, you are revoking the authority you may have unwittingly given to others to determine your identity and destiny. You will also then place yourself in a position to receive God's love which automatically casts out the fear. It is the fear that binds the heart and blocks true openness and forgiveness.

After moving to the side of the road and allowing the other driver to pass, the Lord then spoke to me again. He said, "You are missing many opportunities for intercession, because you continually let others tell you who you are. Then your flesh is busy combating the fear and shame working inside, so that you can't hear My Spirit's prompting you to pray for others." He then went on, "Suppose I told you that the man in the car behind you is someone I love very much. He is very frightened because his wife is in the back seat of his car giving birth to a baby. There are severe complications with the birth, and this man is attempting to rush his wife to the hospital. He is afraid for the life of his wife and their new baby. The devil is indeed trying to kill the wife and the child, and I am trying to get them all to the hospital. You have been in My way!

"I have been looking for someone to intercede in order to release My power into the situation. Now that I have your attention, would you please pull over to the side of the road and pray for this man and his family."

Once I understood the situation, my spirit was really grieved over the way I had acted. I realized what a powerful force fear is and how quickly it can motivate one to idolatry without realizing it. In whatever area you are not totally secure in God's love and care for your life, fear will potentially motivate you to idolatry. Then you are looking to someone or something other than Jesus Christ as the source for your life.

> *"No temptation has overtaken you but such as is common to man; and God is faithful who will not allow you to be tempted beyond what you are able, but with the temptation will provide the way of escape also, that you may be able to endure it. Therefore, my beloved, FLEE IDOLATRY"* (I Corinthians 10:13-14).

There ultimately is really only one sin: IDOLATRY. Every temptation is rooted in idolatry. The way of escape in every temptation is to run to the Lord, ask Him the key questions, establish Jesus Christ as your source, and die to your own flesh's plan to save your soul life. Many Christians have been sorely disappointed waiting for God to extract them from their circumstance, thinking that this will be the way of escape spoken of in this scripture. Many have stopped short at verse 13 and never correlated verse 14 with the previous verse. Fleeing idolatry and running to God is the way of escape that opens the door for God to move in your circumstance and creates the ability for you to forgive your spouse.

If you have found yourself in idolatry toward your husband/wife, perhaps you would like to pray the following prayer to break that idolatry and again establish Jesus as your source of life and the master of your identity and destiny.

Lord God, thank You for exposing the idolatry in my heart. I have allowed my spouse to be the center of my life instead of looking to You. I have granted my spouse authority to determine my identity and destiny and I now see that this is wrong. I repent today of my idolatry toward my spouse, and I ask You, Lord, to forgive me. Cleanse and heal my mind and emotions by the blood of Jesus. Right now I revoke the authority with which I have empowered my husband/wife to tell me who I am, or to determine my future. I grant that authority to You alone Lord Jesus Christ, and I trust You to meet my needs. Please tell me Lord, Who am I in your sight? What does my future look like to You? (Now just wait on Him and let the Lord answer these questions for you).

Who or What Controls Your Life?

In recent years, a book entitled *The 7 Habits of Highly Effective People,*[2] by Stephen R. Covey has become very popular in the business world. In his book, Covey identifies a foundational character quality which he has termed proactivity. Although the focus of Covey's book is primarily on business, I find that this character quality is critical to the restoration of a troubled marriage and is one which we continually see operative in the life of Jesus in the Gospels. For a Christian, this same character quality of proactivity could be termed being led by the Holy Spirit as opposed to being led by the flesh.

Let's now look at this foundational character quality. Are you a proactive or a reactive person? A proactive person makes choices **based on deeply held values,** not based on circumstances, emotions, or the choices of others. A reactive person empowers circumstances, emotions and other people to control his life. He is merely a puppet on the end of a string reacting to what others do and say. A reactive person perceives himself as a victim of life's circumstances and the choices of others, all of which are beyond his control.

A proactive person takes responsibility for his own life and choices. Response-ability really means the ability to choose a response. Proactivity understands that God is the ultimate authority, so nothing anyone else says or does is deterministic in my life, but can only influence me. A proactive person realizes that it is not the circumstances and choices of others that are important in life, but rather **my response** to these things. It is not really what is done to you is what can hurt you, but rather your response to what is done to you is that has far more potential to hurt you.

Jesus said in Mark, chapter 7: *"Listen to me all of you and understand: there is nothing outside a man which going into him can defile him;* ***but the things which proceed out of the man are what defile the man****... For from within, out of the heart of men, proceed the evil thoughts, fornications, thefts, murders, adulteries, deeds of coveting, and wickedness, as well as deceit, sensuality, envy, slander, pride and foolishness. All these evil things proceed from within and defile the man"* (Mark 7:14b-15, 21-23). God looks upon the response of the heart to circumstances, not upon the circumstances themselves. I would put it this way: **How you respond to the people and circumstances of your life today either qualifies or disqualifies you for the future God had in mind for you tomorrow.**

A reactive person does not take responsibility for his life and choices, but rather blames others for his circumstances. He perceives himself as a victim constantly at the mercy of people and forces outside of his control. He perceives that he has no choice and thus takes no response-ability (ability to choose a response) because he has empowered the sin and weaknesses of others to control him and determine the outcome of his life. In reality, as long as you are blaming others and refuse to take responsibility for your own choices, you are not yet positioned for a change in your circumstance. Until you can honestly admit, "I find myself in the circumstance I am in today because of the choices I made yesterday," you cannot yet say, "I choose to respond otherwise." Nobody can **make** you miserable, or angry, or ruin your life. Only you can choose to be miserable, angry, or have your life ruined. The problem is never "out there." The real problem is internal, in your response to people and circumstances. **Any time you think your problem is "out there," <u>that thought is the problem</u>.**

Of course, people's choices can hurt us physically, economically, or emotionally. But they cannot really hurt our identity, destiny or character unless we allow them to do so. Identity and destiny belong to God and character is a product of our choices in response to circumstances of life. In actuality, strong character and emotional freedom come through choosing a right response to life's most difficult circumstances. We have all known and admired people who, in the face of great adversity, have made proactive choices based on deeply held values rather than reactive choices based on fear, pain avoidance, or convenience. Strong character necessary for the future is developed out of our godly responses to difficult circumstances. Thus, your present circumstance, although perhaps designed by Satan, will prove to be God's training ground for your future, if you respond correctly.

A proactive person initiates new behavior and attitudes from the Spirit, while a reactive person simply mirrors the attitudes and behavior coming at him. A proactive person is led by the Spirit of God and yields his mind, will, and emotions to The Holy Spirit in his spirit. A reactive person is led by his flesh and yields his mind, will and emotions to the dictates of his flesh. The enemy will always present to you what appear to be two bad choices. A reactive person feels trapped and doomed to choose one of the two bad choices. A proactive person knows that there is always a third alternative which God will show him as he seeks Him.

In the first chapter of Daniel, Daniel and his friends were offered two bad choices: either violate the dietary laws given to them by God, or violate the king's command to eat his food and suffer the consequences (probably death). As Daniel sought God, God gave him a third alternative which met the goals of God, Daniel and the king. The Pharisees were always trying to trap Jesus between two bad alternatives. Jesus always found a third alternative by initiating entirely new behavior and attitudes in the Spirit.

In Luke 20:19-25, Jesus' enemies asked Him if it were right to pay taxes to Caesar, intending to turn the Jews against Him if He said yes, or turn Him in to the Romans for treason if He said no.

Jesus was not reactive. He initiated a third alternative which was neither of the responses upon which His enemies had counted. He simply asked to see a coin and asked whose picture was on it. When they responded that it was Caesar's, He then told them to give to Caesar that which was his and to God that which was His.

In John 8:3-11, Jesus again was faced with two bad alternatives. His enemies brought Him a woman caught in adultery and asked Him what to do with her. Again Jesus did not react in the flesh, but rather initiated a third alternative from the Spirit. He told them to stone her, but to let the man without sin cast the first stone. Of course, since no one was without sin, there was no one left to stone her. Jesus then forgave the woman and commanded her not to sin any more.

A proactive person's language reflects his responsibility for his own choices based on values he holds. A reactive person's language reflects his empowerment of other people and circumstances to control his life. He is not free to choose. A proactive person may say, "I **choose not to** serve on your committee, as my available time is already committed elsewhere." A reactive person would say, "I **can't** serve on the committee because I don't have time." *I don't control my time. Time controls me*. Proactive: "He deeply hurt me, but **I choose** to forgive him." Reactive: "**He made** me mad. **He ruined** my life." *I'm not responsible. Other people's choices control my emotional well being and the outcome of my life*. Proactive: "I choose, I prefer, I will." Reactive: "He made me, I can't, I have to."

This is a very important area to check regarding your relationship to your spouse. In that relationship, have you been a proactive or a reactive person? Are you free to choose a proper response to your spouse's words and behavior, based on deeply held values or are you just a puppet on a string who is controlled and manipulated by the words and actions of your spouse? Are you free to overcome evil with good (Rom. 12:17-21), or are you compelled to defend and justify yourself every time you are attacked? Is your marriage commitment dependent upon the choices of your spouse, or is it a commitment before God based on biblical values independent of the choices of your spouse? Are your choices predicated upon fear, pain avoidance and convenience, or upon deeply held values which you have received from God? These are penetrating but important questions to ponder as you are considering how to respond to your spouse in your present circumstance. Perhaps you find that you really have been quite reactive rather than proactive in your relationship up until now. Do not despair. God can change this.

Are You Dependent, Independent, or Interdependent?

Stephen Covey goes on in his book to explain that the ability to respond proactively rather than reactively is based upon emotional maturity.[3] Small children are 100% reactive. Their emotions and responses are totally controlled by circumstances and the choices of other people. Many adults have not really grown emotionally much past this stage of development. If you find it very difficult not to respond reactively, you may need to ask the Lord to help you mature emotionally. Covey identifies three basic stages of emotional maturity. You must progress through each stage in order to move on to the next stage. These stages are: Dependent, Independent, and Interdependent. Both dependent and independent people tend to be quite reactive. Let's look at some of the characteristics of this emotional maturity continuum.

Dependent: A dependent person tends to be **"you" centered.** He has primarily empowered other people to control his life, and needs others to accomplish his goals. He tends to be very self centered and wants others to orient their lives around meeting his needs. When they don't, he feels like a victim and deals with lots of anger, self pity, discouragement and depression. The dependent person does not take responsibility for his choices, but, instead, blames others for the things that don't work in his life. He doesn't keep many of his commitments, because circumstances and the choices of others always preclude this. He is a short-term thinker and usually does not see the sowing and reaping cycle of the choices made today (seed) creating the circumstances he will face tomorrow (fruit). Most of the dependent person's choices are based on fear, emotions and short-term pain avoidance.

Independent: An independent person is **"I" centered**. He has empowered himself to control his life and doesn't need others to accomplish his goals. He has made himself the master of his own destiny and usually takes great pride in doing so. Since he has decided that he really does not need other people, relationships are really only a means to an end. Like the dependent person, the independent person is also very self centered, and thus has very little sensitivity to the needs of others around him. He oftentimes struggles with pride, arrogance, and loneliness. He has very few, true friends or meaningful relationships. He recognizes a measure of responsibility for his choices, but may abandon commitments in the name of independence. When others won't help him, or do what he wants, he reacts by simply writing them off, and moving on, relying upon himself to meet his own needs. Most of the independent person's choices are primarily driven by fear, pride, and frequently, rebellion.

Interdependent: The interdependent person is **"we" centered**. He has progressed through the independent stage and has come to recognize that he is not the center of the universe, but rather that God is. He has come to recognize his own need for others, but does not empower the choices of others to control his life or emotional well-being. He is not relying on either self effort or the choices of others to accomplish his goals. He has actually forsaken his own goals all together and is now living to see the will of God accomplished in his life and the lives of all others around him. The interdependent person has empowered God to be the master of his destiny and, as such, is no longer compelled either to use others, or isolate from others, in order to protect or care for himself. He believes that God knows him, loves him, and will care for his well-being. Therefore he is free to concern himself with the needs of others and combine his efforts with them to accomplish the will of God. He is proactive and takes responsibility for the choices he makes. He recognizes that his success is dependent upon making others successful, and so his primary focus is on how to meet the needs and goals of others. He recognizes that external stimuli influence his life, but do not control it. His choices are thus based on deeply held internal values rather than on feelings, circumstances, the choices of others, or short-term pain avoidance.

It is important to take a look at your own life to see where along the emotional maturity continuum you primarily tend to operate. If you find yourself primarily dependent, then you will want to pray for the Lord to begin to teach you how to grow into independence, and then on into interdependence. If you find yourself independent, then you will want to pray for the Lord to teach you how to transfer your trust for your well- being from yourself and your own efforts to Him, so that you can grow up into interdependence. In this way, you can learn to make wise, proactive choices, based on true biblical values regarding your life and your marriage partner.

Are You a Flea or a Battery?

I have found over the years that many people establish the foundation of their marriage upon emotional dependence toward each other, rather than interdependence. Most people, when they were in search of a marriage partner, could be likened to a flea. A flea is a small animal in search of a large dog. The dream of every flea is to find a large dog upon whom the flea can alight and draw life. The dog has so much life that it does not even miss the life that the flea draws. Most people, upon discovering their marriage partner, thought that they had found the ultimate big dog. "Just being with her makes me feel so wonderful," he would say. "He is such a gentleman. When I am with him, I feel so secure and protected," she would say. Each person thought that they had found a wonderful dog who continually gave them pleasure and life and required very little in return.

However, shortly after the wedding, a great revelation came to most of us. "The person I have married is not in reality even a dog at all, but is actually another flea." Now we have two fleas and no dog. Both fleas are trying to draw the life out of each other, but no one has any life. This is a picture of two emotionally dependent, highly reactive people who have established a foundation in their personal lives and now also in their marriage which is certain to result in the collapse of the structure built upon such a foundation.

Let me give you another picture of two, interdependent people in a marriage relationship. This is a picture of two rechargeable batteries. A battery does not ever ask the radio it is called to energize to give back to it. The battery does not ever say to the radio, "Hey, radio, all I've been doing around here is serving you and giving you life. Where's mine? When are you going to give some life back to me?" No! The battery just continues to give life unilaterally to the radio. When the battery runs out of life, it never looks to the radio, but instead goes back to the recharger. Jesus Christ, of course, in this picture, is the recharger. If each partner is only looking to give life to the other partner and is looking to Jesus to receive life, then there is a tremendous synergy which begins to take place in such a marriage.

Some think that it would take both partners to produce this, but, in actuality, it takes only one to start it. However, it does take someone who can operate in emotional interdependence to make a series of proactive choices. Only a proactive person can be a battery. Reactive persons are all doomed to be fleas until they can recognize their emotional immaturity, repent, and begin to let God grow them up.

Many times the emotional response patterns and growth are directly correlatable with the way people were treated in growing up years. Frequently, there are generational patterns which repeat themselves as children grow into adulthood, and marry. Many people can see similar patterns being repeated in their own marriages and lives which they saw in their parents. These cycles do not have to be repeated. They can be broken. If these patterns, which oftentimes result in shame, anger, strife, abuse, sexual immorality, divorce, etc. are not dealt with and broken in the present generation, they will tend to pass right on down to the next generation, resulting in your children's having to deal with intensified versions of the same sort of devastation. We have designed a three day seminar to deal with such issues, entitled **FAMILY FOUNDATIONS BASIC SEMINAR**. This seminar deals with generational patterns, reasons for emotional immaturity, how parents can be either agents of God or Satan in imparting identity and destiny to their children, relational communication in marriage and many other topics. For more information on how you can participate in a *Family Foundations Basic Seminar* in your area, see page 137 in the back of this book.

Do You Growl, Moan, or Pray?

One other foundational area that is good to check is your response to injustice. Many people struggle greatly in dealing with injustice more than they do with other difficult circumstances. The Prophet Isaiah describes three basic responses to injustice in Isaiah 59.

> *"All of us growl like bears, and moan sadly like doves;*
> *We hope for justice, but there is none, for salvation, but*

> *it is far from us. For our transgressions are multiplied before Thee, and our sins testify against us, and we know our iniquities; Transgressing and denying the Lord, and turning away from our God, speaking oppression and revolt, conceiving in and uttering from the heart lying words. And justice is turned back, and righteousness stands far away; For truth has stumbled in the street, and uprightness cannot enter. Yes, truth is lacking; And he who turns aside from evil makes himself a prey. Now the Lord saw, and it was displeasing in His sight that there was no justice. And He saw that there was no man and was astonished that there was no one to intercede;"* (Isa. 59:11-16b).

There are two, primary, reactive responses of the flesh to injustice: fight or flight. Isaiah here describes them as either growling like a bear or moaning sadly like a dove. If you feel that your spouse has betrayed you or treated you unfairly, you will be tempted to either growl or moan. You may want either to get angry and attack or sink into a pit of self pity and mope. Neither of these responses is helpful or changes anything for the good. Isaiah here also outlines one other response which has a chance of actually changing things. This response is to intercede in prayer.

When we get wounded, there is a lot of emotional energy which usually builds up inside us. This energy needs to be expended in some way. Some people try to stuff it deep inside and pretend that the wound does not exist. This is not healthy, and it will either blow out in anger, depression, or some other form at a later date, or the body will absorb it and potentially cause all manner of sickness. Other people simply vent their emotional energy on others, which is perhaps healthier for them in the short run, but destroys relationship with those upon whom they vent. Actually, as I shared in the beginning of this chapter, Jesus Christ is the only

One in the universe upon Whom you can vent without significantly damaging relationship. This is why the prophet Isaiah says that God is actually astonished that He can find no one to intercede.

The third response of the Spirit to injustice is to intercede in prayer. This is a very good use of the pent up emotional energy. Recognize that your husband/wife is not the enemy, no matter how much he/she may be acting as such. The true enemy is Satan and his demonic host who are working very hard to establish strongholds of deception both in you and in your spouse. These need to be torn down in prayer. Prayer is a place in which you can release as much emotional energy as you want without damaging any relationships. God is very secure in His own identity. He is not threatened by your anger and finds no need to defend Himself when you feel that He or others are not treating you fairly. Thus you want to check your own heart to see if you have been a growler, moaner or one who intercedes when injustice has been perpetrated against you.

Before there is much hope for God to rebuild your marriage, you must first examine your own heart and allow God to expose the wrong foundations there, and then let God rebuild in these areas. As the rubble is cleared away from your own life, then it is far more possible for God to rebuild in your spouse's life and marriage relationship. Let's review the areas we have been examining in this chapter. Honestly rate your responses in the following areas on a scale of 1 to 5 (5 being a spiritual response and 1 being a fleshly response).

Do you have a heart that seeks after God first or one that seeks after your spouse first? ________

Have you recognized that your battle is not against your spouse, but rather against Satan and his spiritual forces of wickedness and fought accordingly? ________

Have you been a proactive or a reactive person? ________

Have you been more of a flea or a battery toward your spouse? ________

When you have been unjustly and unfairly treated do you tend to growl like a bear, moan sadly like a dove, or release your frustration to God and intercede in prayer? ________

Have you been in idolatry toward your spouse, empowering him/her to determine your identity and destiny? ________

Have you experienced difficulty being able to truly forgive your spouse from your heart due to the above mentioned idolatry? ________

Have you empowered the weaknesses and sin of your spouse to control your life and emotional well-being? ________

Are your choices based upon your spouse's choices or are you free to initiate Spirit-led choices based on deeply held values? ________

As you honestly examine your emotional responses to your spouse, do you find yourself more dependent, independent or interdependent? ________

As you honestly have evaluated some of the foundations of your own life and relationship, you may have found that much of your life and marital relationship have been built on sand. If you found that you had to honestly give yourself a lot of 1's and 2's in answer to the above questions, be encouraged. Upon knowing this it is now possible to begin to clear away the rubble, go to God and ask Him to help you rebuild first your life and then your marriage relationship on the Rock, Jesus Christ, His love and His Word. You will need some help and support in doing so. I encourage you to speak with your pastor about counseling you or helping you to find a godly counselor who can help you through this process. Another very excellent ministry which I highly recommend is *Covenant Keepers*.[4] This is a Christian ministry specifically geared to help and support those who are separated or divorced from a marriage partner. Call the phone number listed at the end of this page to find a ministry support group in your local area.

---

[1]Phillipps, Marilyn, *First Aid for a Wounded Marriage*, Littleton: Eden Publishing, 1992, (303) 730-3333

[2]Covey, Stephen R., *The 7 Habits of Highly Effective People*, New York: Simon & Schuster, 1989

[3]*ibib*. pp. 40-51.

[4]***Covenant Keepers***, P.O. Box 702371, Tulsa, Oklahoma 74170-2371, Phone: (918) 743-0365

Chapter 2

Principals, Values & Strategies

In the last chapter, we talked about allowing God to rebuild in us some foundational character qualities, particularly regarding how we respond to people and circumstances in life. In this chapter we want to examine some foundational values upon which God can rebuild your life and marriage. Out of these key values, a practical strategy of how to respond and relate to your spouse can be developed.

We previously talked about the importance of living a proactive, rather than a reactive life. We said that a proactive person bases his choices on **deeply held values**, not on circumstances, emotions, or the choices of others. Many people are not able to live a proactive life because they have never stopped to consider what values they really do hold. Obviously you cannot live your life taking responsibility for choices based on deeply held values if you have never identified any deeply held values.

What is a value anyway? We will define the word value here for our usage as: "my understanding of a true and correct principle of life to which I ascribe great nobility, importance, worth and esteem." Values are my understanding of those principles of life which I hold to be important and worthy of being the foundation of my life. Thus, again, in order to make my choices based on values, I must have thought through and understood what principles I do deeply value.

Once I have identified my basic values, I can then establish the purpose and vision of my life which will be a reflection of the values I hold. I can then set goals and develop strategies to accomplish the purposes and vision of my life. Unfortunately, one who has not thought through and established his own values, purposes and strategies will, by default, end up being controlled by, and simply a reactor to, the values, purposes, and strategies of other people, and ultimately of the kingdom of darkness. All people actually do hold values whether they have ever thought about it or not, but only one who knows and understands the values he does hold can develop a proactive strategy of life.

Some people have thought through their values, but the values which they hold are not consistent with true principles of life. Values are based on principles, but are not in and of themselves principles. A principle is the reality of how life actually is. A value is my understanding of a principle. For example, gravity is a consistent principle of life on planet Earth. Most people hold a value that gravity will rapidly attract any free object toward the planet's surface. As a result of this value, most people have established a life strategy of not stepping off cliffs or tall buildings.

Principles, values and strategies, could be likened to the following analogy. Suppose I intend to drive across a specific territory from one point to another. Principles are the actual land. Values are the map of the land, and strategies are my plans of how I will actually cross the land. Obviously the closer my map is to the actual lay of the land, the more success I will have in implementing a strategy to cross the land. Suppose that my map shows a paved highway spanning a 100-mile stretch of land. I thus choose a strategy of simply driving my car along the highway to reach my destination. As I set out, I find that 20 miles down the road the pavement terminates in a lake which was not shown on my map. I have obviously chosen at this point an ineffective strategy to arrive at my destination.

The closer one's values are aligned with true principles, the more success one will enjoy in developing strategies to handle life's circumstances that actually do work. If you hold a value that gravity is only operative six days a week and does not function on Saturdays, you may then establish a practice of jumping off cliffs on Saturdays. Since your value is not aligned with the reality of the principle of gravity, your practice will most likely result in death or serious injury.

As a practical example, most Christians hold a value that their belief in the death and resurrection of Jesus Christ and their trust in Him as Savior and Lord will result in their sins being forgiven and their being raised from the dead to eternal life with Christ. In I Corinthians 15, Apostle Paul tells us that this value is indeed in line with the reality of life, but if it were not, then we above all people are most to be pitied. In other words, no matter how important the value is to you, or how many people believe it, or how long it has been accepted as a correct value, if it is ever found not to line up with truth, throw it out, or modify it to conform to truth. Paul says, basically, that if we ever find that in reality the dead are not raised and therefore Jesus has not been raised from the dead, then we ought to quit hoping in Jesus. But he goes on to say that the dead are indeed raised and thus our value is truly in alignment with reality and thus we are right to hope in Christ.

> *"For if the dead are not raised, not even Christ has been raised; and if Christ has not been raised, your faith is worthless; you are still in your sins. Then those also who have fallen asleep in Christ have perished. If we have*

hoped in Christ in this life only, we are of all men most to be pitied" I Cor. 15:16-19.

In order to develop an effective strategy for relating to your spouse and your present marital circumstance, I believe it is important to first examine three basic values. This may seem somewhat elementary, but I have found that many people have not ever really examined their own values regarding marriage, or their marriage partner. As a result, such a person is doomed to be a reactive puppet controlled by Satan through the choices and agendas of a spouse and other people.

How Do You Determine Truth?

The first value which we will examine has to do with your methodology for determining truth. How do you determine which principles are truth and reality so that you can establish your values based on true principles? Many people use many different methods for determining truth. Some people base truth upon their life experience; others upon the opinions of the majority of their friends and those whom they respect. Others base truth upon their father's opinions or those of a respected mentor, pastor, or spiritual leader. Some people determine truth based upon what is written by "experts" in books, upon the TV and media opinion, upon tradition, or the long-standing opinion of their church. Others base truth upon their subjective experience of dreams, visions, prophetic words, or their personally hearing the voice of the Lord.

All of these are valid and helpful ways to lead one toward truth, some more so than others. However, all of these methods have a significant element of subjectivity in them and may or may not be rooted in objective, absolute truth and reality. Jesus Christ said in the Gospel of John the following words:

> "***I am** the way, and the truth and the life; no one comes to the Father, but through Me*" (John 14:6).

> "*Jesus therefore was saying to those Jews who had believed in Him, 'If you abide in My word, then you are truly disciples of Mine; and you shall know the truth and the truth shall make your free'*" (John 8:31-32).

Jesus here declares that He is the truth, and that if we abide in His Word we will know the truth and will be set free by it. I would here propose that the Bible in general, and the words of Jesus Christ in specific, are the prime objective bases for determining truth. It is further spoken of Jesus that He is the Word of God. "*In the beginning was the Word and the Word was with God and the Word was God. ...And the Word became flesh and dwelt among us,*" (John 1:1, 14a). Since Jesus is both the Word and truth, when we embrace and abide in His Word, we embrace and abide in Him and in truth.

> "***All scripture is inspired by God** and profitable for teaching, for reproof, for correction, for training in righteousness; that the man of God may be adequate, equipped for every good work*" (II Tim. 3:16).

> "*But know this first of all, that no prophecy of Scripture is a matter of one's own interpretation, for **no prophecy was ever made by an act of human will, but men moved by the Holy Spirit spoke from God***" (II Peter 1:20-21).

As a follower of Jesus Christ, I hold a deep value that the Bible is the inspired Word of God. It is the product of hand-picked men who spoke and wrote as they were moved upon by the Holy

Spirit, and I accept the Bible as my infallible guide in matters pertaining to conduct and doctrine. This means that I grant the Bible authority to govern what I believe and how I live. If there is a conflict between a circumstance and the Word of God, I will put my faith in the Word of God and expect the circumstance to change and line up with the Word of God, rather than accept the circumstance as truth and ignore or change the Word of God.

It is beyond the scope of this book to discuss in detail how one can know that the Bible is really the Word of God, that it is accurate and you can rely upon it. For more understanding on this topic, see the list suggested at the end of this chapter for further reading.[1] It is only my intention here to stimulate your thinking to consider what value you hold regarding the authority of the Word of God in your life.

The reason that it is important to consider our value for the Word of God is that there has been a significant value exchange in the Church regarding the Bible over the last 50 years or so. It used to be that Christians accepted the Bible as the infallible Word and will of God and it was enough to simply state what the Bible said as a basis of right or wrong behavior. Christians used to consider the Word of God as an absolute which was not questioned.

However, in this century, especially with the advent of modern science, men have learned to question everything until it is proven experientially. Consequently, **the former value of the absoluteness of the Word of God has been exchanged for the value of the Word of God being relative** like everything else, only to be believed and accepted as authoritative in one's life upon being proven experientially. The problem with this value is that many individuals and families are perishing as Christians are experimenting with the violation of basic life principles. Unfortunately, many do not discover the consequences of violating basic scriptural principles until after tremendous damage is already done, not only to themselves, but also to children and other related parties.

How do you determine truth? Are the words of Jesus Christ an authoritative source of truth for your life? Is the Bible the Word of God, which is absolute, doesn't change and can be relied upon as a basis of conduct and doctrine? Do you believe that God's Word is an expression of God's will for your life? Do you believe that faith toward God in believing His Word has creative power to impact, influence, and change natural circumstances?

If you hold a value for the Word of God, as I do, which answers all of these questions in the affirmative, then you will have a strong basis for constructing a strategy in relating to your spouse which is based on the value that the Bible is the Word of God and that the Word of God is true. If, on the other hand, you do not hold such a value for the Word of God, then you will have to construct a different strategy than the one I will suggest which is based on the above stated value. It is never fruitful for a person to attempt to implement a strategy of conduct inconsistent with his own inherent values. However, if you hold a value that the Word of God is true, then you have a strong basis for faith that God will act totally consistently with His Word and that your strategy to implement His goals (not yours) will bear fruit.

Self-sacrifice vs. Selfishness

Let us now turn our attention to a second foundational value which has also been exchanged in the Church in this century. Most Christians have **exchanged the former value of self-sacrificial living for the value of selfish living.** One hundred years ago, because this value was commonly held, virtually every child had a Father, a Family, and a Future. This is not necessarily true today. In those days, people recognized the corporate good as more valuable than the individual good. Families, communities, and even nations banded together in cooperation, many times with great self sacrifice, for the corporate good. This value is still held today in Middle Eastern cultures. It is not difficult in many Arab nations to find volunteers for suicide missions for the corporate good of the people group or religion. In our western culture today, we would not find many who would be willing to die for a country or culture. I dare say that we would not yet even find many who would be willing to die for Jesus Christ.

In times past, self-sacrificial living was held among Christians as a deep value. Jesus gave up His life for us, therefore we ought to be willing to give up our lives on behalf of others. I know that this sounds very strange in the light of most of the teaching in the last 30 years. The primary teaching has been that God wants to bless and prosper me. The reason Jesus died, we have been taught, is so that I might prosper and be blessed. God certainly does want to bless and prosper us, but the end result is not for us. It is meant to be a pass-through to others. God told Abraham in Genesis 12 that He would bless and prosper him beyond measure, but that the end result was that He wished to bless all the families of the earth through Abraham. In other words, Abraham's blessing was not just for him, but was meant to bring blessing to all the families of the earth.

Because of the recent emphasis on blessing and prosperity in the body of Christ, many people have forsaken the value of self-sacrificial living and instead have embraced the value of selfish living. I don't think that most of the Bible teachers have taught selfishness, but because of the emphasis, many people have received prosperity teaching in this way. This has discredited much of our message in the sight of the watching world, as the entire world knows that self sacrifice is a virtue and selfishness is sin. This is why, even in the world, people listen to Mother Theresa and admire her, while Jim Bakker is mocked and sentenced to prison. When an airplane crashes or a fire breaks out in a building, the world doesn't exalt and put on national news those who used all their energy and faith to save themselves and left others to die. No, there is no virtue perceived in that. Rather, it is those who, at the risk of their own lives, did not flee, but used their energy and faith to save others. Thus there is an inherent recognized value in self sacrifice. This, of course, is the true message of the Gospel. This is what Jesus did for all of us.

Historically, families lived together, ate together, and worked together. Corporate survival of the family was a major issue. Children did not have a choice as to whether they wanted to get up at 4:30 a.m. and milk the cows or not. They realized that if they did not, the entire family would suffer and perhaps eventually perish. In modern times the past value of corporate physical survival has been replaced by individual emotional survival. Each person carries so much emotional pain and damage that the goal of many is simply to survive, and as much as possible, avoid further emotional pain. This way of thinking, of course, retains one in the emotionally immature state of dependence, making one reactive instead of proactive. Such a person is then kept as a victim of circumstances and the choices of others, which continues to generate abundant emotional pain.

As this basic value exchange has taken place, many Christians have become like crabs. I am told that it is very simple to retain crabs once caught. You see, crabs have no sense of corporate welfare, as each crab acts only on its own behalf. Thus when many crabs are put in a pot or bucket together, it is not necessary to secure the container with a lid. The crabs, themselves, will not let any one crab escape. If one crab should climb up to the top of the container and seek to escape, all the other crabs will grab hold of him and pull him back down into the bucket with them. Since they cannot all escape at once, none of them can escape.

My greatest concern is not that this value exchange has taken place in the world, but that the Church has embraced the same value exchange. Selfish thinking and living are just as rampant in the Church as they are among those outside the Church. We, in the Church, are meant to be salt and light to the world around us. When we have lost our saltiness, then there is nothing on the earth to hinder the destruction and societal deterioration which the kingdom of darkness continues to perpetrate amongst us.

Why are You Here?

One of the prime results of this value exchange is that children growing up in this environment have lost the sense of intrinsic worth and destiny. In times past, each person growing up felt unique and special. He felt valuable to God and to society, as though he were here for a purpose far greater than himself and that he had something unique to contribute to society and to the kingdom of God. It was not that long ago that young people used to experience a sense of destiny and reason to live far beyond themselves. I recently read a letter which my father wrote to his father in 1942, explaining his future plans after the war. My father grew up in a traditional, denominational church and thus did not have at this point in his life a strong sense of being led by the Lord. However, it is interesting to note the values he held as a 20-year-old man in 1942. I would like to quote a portion of this letter below.

"Dear Dad,

As an outgrowth of our short talk on occupational interests this afternoon, I would like to indicate my plans for the future to avoid misunderstandings...

After the war I plan to return to school to study many different scientific, military, and political fields. My main interests lie in the many fields of science such as medicine, genetics, physics, chemistry, astronomy; and certain scientific, psychological, mental effects connected with medicine. The only reason that I would go into politics or military affairs is if they are as corrupt as they have been so many times in the past. That is, if we win the war and lose the peace so as to find ourselves in just as bad a position as if Germany had won the war, then it would seem necessary to go into a political war against these darn political ring leaders that frequently run our congress. In my case I don't give a darn about money. As long as I can get enough to eat and a little clothes to wear, I will spend the rest of the time wherever it can do the most good, whether its fighting international military wars, or fighting political ring leaders, or trying to lick some baffling scientific problems...

After the war I plan to go back to school for the rest of my life to study and try to solve as many of these problems as possible. This work, of course, pays very little, so financially I plan to be practically dead broke all of my life. If a person works with a University you will perhaps receive 4 or 5 thousand dollars per year after considerable number of years of experience, but at the same time you are perhaps buying 3 or 4 thousand dollars worth of equipment for your research that your department couldn't afford to buy for you. This, perhaps, leaves you with less than $1000 per year. All in all, you can only expect to barely make a living & never save up any money. That's just the type of work I like in that I detest high salary men that keep spending their money on themselves or feathering their own nests. This is a field that you can really be a service to your country-men to develop methods & apparatus for relieving pain and curing the diseased." (Gilman Hill, July 26,1942)

The thing that was shocking to me was the sense of destiny and purpose beyond himself that my father possessed as a twenty-year-old. He definitely held the value of self-sacrifice far above self-gratification. His purpose was to be of service to his countrymen, have enough food and clothing to live and then spend the rest of his time wherever it could do the most good. After reading this letter, I asked my father if this was an unusual attitude which he uniquely possessed. He told me that this was not unique at all. Most of his friends and those with whom he was in school all had a similar attitude. Apparently at that time there was a value held by many people of self-sacrificial living for the good of society and others. This value has all but departed as a lifestyle from our present society. This is something which I believe that God is wanting to restore to His Church.

As you consider how you will relate to your spouse and your present circumstance, this fundamental value must be examined. For whom are you living? Are you living for Jesus Christ, His name, His kingdom, His will and for the benefit and welfare of your children and others who don't know Him; or are you living for yourself, your short-term happiness and emotional well being? Do you embrace the basic value of self-sacrificial living or the value of selfish living? These questions are critical for you to answer in your own heart before God.

For a Christian, happiness is not really the goal of life. In the Kingdom of God the goal is obedience to Jesus and the expansion and promotion of His Kingdom. Joy and fulfillment of life are not the goals, but rather are the by-products that come from serving Jesus. One who seeks the by-product rather than the goal usually misses out on both. Jesus said that seeking your own pleasure and happiness will cause you to lose the very thing you are seeking.

> "*If anyone wishes to come after* Me, *let him deny himself, and take up his cross, and follow* Me. *For whoever wishes to save his own life shall lose it; but whoever loses his life for* My *sake and the gospel's shall save it*" (Mark 8:34-35).

So serving Jesus and serving self are opposite goals and are incompatible with each other. Serving Jesus is based on the value of self-sacrifice, and serving self is based on the value of self-gratification. God has never forced anyone to serve Him. It is a free choice for each of us. However, we must recognize that there is a choice, and again our strategies must be based on the actual values we really do hold.

Marriage: Covenant or Contract?

The third critical value which we will examine in this chapter has to do with your value of marriage as an institution of God. Do you view marriage as a covenant or as a contract? Again there has been a value exchange in the last 50 years regarding marriage. In past times, most of western society considered marriage a covenant relationship. Over the past fifty years, a value exchange has taken place to the point that in the mid 1990's even most of the Church accepts the value that marriage is a contract. Let me further explain these terms "contract" and "covenant." Many people are not aware that there is a conceptual difference between a contract and a covenant.

Covenant (often times referred to as "blood covenant") is an eastern concept which has been known and practiced for centuries in the East, but is little known nor understood in the West. The Bible is set in an eastern context, and much of the biblical presentation of God's relationship with man is couched in covenant terminology. Unfortunately, most of us in the West have very little familiarity even with the concept of covenant. The closest most of us have come to the concept of covenant is watching Geronomo make a blood covenant with another Indian chief on TV when we were children and then pricking our own finger with a friend in order to become blood brothers.

A blood covenant is actually the closest, most sacred, most enduring, binding agreement known to men. Such a covenant is virtually never broken by those who understand and practice blood covenanting. It is such a sacred commitment that a man would die before he would dishonor himself by breaking a covenant. In the

East, a man's word in a vow or covenant was more valuable than his life. It is said that 100 years ago if a man ever broke a covenant in Africa, even his own relatives would help hunt him down to kill him. He and his offspring would be hunted and killed for up to four generations for covenant breaking. It is said that among North American Indian peoples that a covenant breaker was hunted and killed for up to seven generations.

H. Clay Trumbull, a biblical and anthropological scholar wrote a fascinating book in the early 1890's entitled, *The Blood Covenant.* In this work, Dr. Trumbull expounds upon the cultural traditions of blood covenanting in virtually every culture of the world. It is his thesis that God placed such traditions in each culture to prepare every people group in the world to understand the New Covenant God has made with man by the shedding of the blood of Jesus Christ. Below, I would like to quote a couple brief passages from Dr. Trumbull's book to give you an idea of how men in the past have made blood covenants with each other.

"In bringing this rite of the covenant of blood into new prominence, it may be well for me to tell of it as it was described to me by an intelligent native Syrian, who saw it consummated in a village at the base of the mountains of Lebanon;...

"It was two young men, who were to enter into this covenant. They had known each other, and had been intimate (He does not mean sexually), *for years; but now they were to become brother-friends, in covenant of blood. Their relatives and neighbors were called together, in the open place before the village fountain, to witness the sealing compact. The young men publicly announced their purpose, and their reasons for it. Their declarations were written down, in duplicate—one paper for each friend—and signed by themselves and by several witnesses. One of the friends took a sharp lancet, and opened a vein in the other's arm. Into the opening thus made, he inserted a quill, through which he sucked the living blood. The lancet-blade was carefully wiped on one of the duplicate covenant-papers, and then it was taken by the other friend, who made a*

like incision in its first user's arm, and drank his blood through the quill, wiping the blade on the duplicate covenant-record. The two friends declared together: 'We are brothers in a covenant made before God: who deceiveth the other, him will God deceive.' Each blood-marked covenant-record was then folded carefully, to be sewed up in a small leathern case, or amulet, about an inch square; to be worn thenceforward by one of the covenant-brothers, suspended about the neck, or bound upon the arm, in token of ***the indissoluble relation***.”[2] (See Exodus 13:16).

Dr. Trumbull further states: “*He who has entered into this compact with another, counts himself the possessor of a double life;* ***for his friend, whose blood he has shared, is ready to lay down his life with him, or for him***.”[3] Dr. Trumbull then refers to the scripture verse, Proverbs 18:24: “*A man of many friends comes to ruin, but there is* ***a friend who sticks closer than a brother***.” This scripture is obviously referring to a blood-covenant brother, as Dr. Trumbull has just described. Jonathan and David made such a covenant with each other as recorded in I Samuel 18.

> “*Now it came about that when he had finished speaking to Saul, that the soul of Jonathan was knit to the soul of David, and Jonathan loved him as himself. And Saul took him that day and did not let him return to his father's house. Then Jonathan made a covenant with David because he loved him as himself. And Jonathan stripped himself of the robe that was on him and gave it to David with his armor, including his sword and his bow and his belt*” (I Samuel 18:1-4).

These types of understandings still exist in oriental and middle eastern cultures today. This is why it is still such a serious matter in many countries for an Arab Muslim to become a Christian. In their way of thinking, the man is in covenant through Islam with God and his brothers. In becoming a Christian, according to eastern thinking, a man is breaking this covenant with God and his brothers and thus is worthy of death. In many cultures, his own mother is sworn to seek his death. Covenant is an irrevocable, indissoluble commitment, breakable only by death. Covenant breaking in the East is virtually always punishable by death. When men made such a covenant with each other, they made a commitment to each other more valuable than even their own lives. When entering into such a covenant, they made the basic commitment to each other that, "all I have and all I am is yours. Your enemies are my enemies, and I am ready to give up even my life for you, if need be."

It is an astounding thing that Almighty God would make covenant with man, committing all He is and all He has to us. Jesus Christ took upon Himself the punishment for our covenant breaking in His establishment of the New Covenant and offered to all who will receive an irrevocable, indissoluble covenant commitment.

The concept of covenant then, is a unilateral, irrevocable, indissoluble commitment before God, valid at least until death. Covenant does not depend upon the performance of either party. Covenant is a unilateral commitment made to another party in the presence of God and is independent of the performance of the other party.

This means that if a man gave his word in covenant, his fulfillment of that word was not dependent upon whether the other man fulfilled his word or not. It was a unilateral commitment before God. In other words, each man had chosen in advance to live a proactive life, not dependent upon the choices of others, but rather dependent upon unilateral choices and commitments made before God. Because of this understanding, it was very rare for an eastern man to ever break a covenant, and if someone did, the entire society was outraged and all were committed to impose upon the covenant breaker the penalty for such behavior, death. It is amazing to note that in ancient Israel, even when a covenant was entered into with purposeful deceit perpetrated by one party against the other, once the covenant vow was made, even after the deceit was discovered, the honorable men of Israel still fulfilled their covenant vow to a deceitful, heathen nation. This story is recorded in the ninth chapter of the book of Joshua.

Joshua Kept His Word

God had instructed Joshua and the Israelites to eliminate from the land all the Canaanites living there. They had already totally annihilated the cities of Jericho and Ai, and were now nearing the Hivite city of Gibeon. The Gibeonites had heard what had been done to Jericho and Ai and were greatly frightened. The elders of the city devised a plan to deceive Joshua and induce him to enter into a covenant of peace with them. They knew that if they could get the Israelites to enter into a covenant with them, they would then be bound to do them no harm.

The Gibeonites sent an envoy to the Israelite camp with worn-out shoes and clothing, stale bread, and cracked and mended wineskins to make it appear as if they had traveled a very great distance. They arrived and appeared before Joshua in this condition and sought to enter into a covenant of peace, saying that they were not inhabitants of the land of Canaan, but rather lived a very great distance away. Joshua and the elders of Israel did not seek the counsel of the Lord, but rather believed the Gibeonites and cut a covenant of peace with them. Only three days later, Joshua discovered that the Gibeonites had deceived him and were occupants of the land of Canaan. Although all of Israel would have liked to destroy the Gibeonites, Joshua and the leaders prevented them because of the covenant which was made with them.

> *"So the men of Israel took some of their provisions and did not ask for the counsel of the Lord. And Joshua made peace with them and made a covenant with them, to let them live, and the leaders of the congregation swore an oath to them. And it came about at the end of three days after they had made a covenant with them, that they heard that they were neighbors and that they were living within their land. Then the sons of Israel set out and came to their cities on the third day. Now their cities were Gibeon, and Chephirah and Beeroth and Kiriath-jearim. And the sons of Israel did not strike them because the leaders of the congregation had sworn to them by the Lord, the God of Israel. And the whole congregation grumbled against the leaders. But all the leaders said to the whole congregation, 'We have sworn to them by the Lord, the God of Israel, and now we cannot touch them. Thus we will so do to them, even let them live, lest wrath be on us for the oath which we swore to them'"* (Joshua 9:14-19).

Despite the fact that it was a covenant that was never meant to be and even was entered into through fraud and deception, once it was made, the Israelites were bound to honor it. Joshua and his leaders understood the issue of covenant and its value before God. They could not break their covenant even though it was made in deception with heathen Canaanites whom God had commanded the Israelites to destroy.

Joshua's concept of covenant was so strong that not only did he preserve the Gibeonites, but in Joshua, chapter 10, he and the Israelites fought alongside the Gibeonites to help defeat their enemies. God so honored the value of this covenant that He placed it even above the individual welfare of His chosen people, Israel. In II Samuel, chapter 21, a famine had been released upon

Israel. When King David inquired of the Lord as to the cause of the famine, the Lord informed him that it was a result of King Saul's having violated the covenant by putting the Gibeonites to death. The famine was terminated only as King David went to the Gibeonites and repented and made restitution for the rebellious acts of former King Saul. We see here again the incredible value God places on covenant as He honors and calls Israel to honor a covenant that should have never been made in the first place.

> "*When you make a vow to God, do not be late in paying it, for He takes no delight in fools. Pay what you vow*" (i.e. Annanias & Saphira, Acts 5). "*It is better that you should not vow than that you should vow and not pay. Do not let your speech cause you to sin and do not say in the presence of the messenger of God that it was a mistake. Why should God be angry on account of your voice and destroy the work of your hands?*" (Ecclesiastes 5:4-6).

How Was a Covenant Made?

Let us now briefly examine the components of a traditional eastern covenant ceremony. The following seven components were usually included:

1. Unilateral commitment before God: The two parties would make a commitment to each other which was unilateral (not dependent upon the fulfillment by the other party), and spoken to and in the presence of God.

2. Terms expressed: The terms of the covenant were specified including duration, and scope of commitment. Most frequently when men would become blood brothers in covenant with each other, the duration was not only until death of the two covenanting

partners, but frequently extended for several generations. God says that His covenant lasts to 1000 generations (Psalm 105:8-10). David's covenant with Jonathan lasted at least through the next generation, as he sought out and blessed Mephibosheth, Jonathan's son, for the sake of covenant with Jonathan (II Samuel 9). Most covenants extend at least until death of the covenanting partners. The scope of the covenant among blood covenant friends would entail a commitment of all available resources up to and including one's own life. "All I have and all I am is yours," was the commitment that was made. This again is the commitment which God makes to us in Christ.

3. Exchange of gifts: Men would traditionally exchange four very valuable gifts as earnest commitment of their sincerity toward God and one another. These four gifts were:

A. Their coats or robes. The coat signified the tribe, standing within the tribe, and was representative of tribal and family identity and authority. To give a man your coat was to give him the benefits (inheritance, etc.) and standing which you enjoy in the nation, tribe and family.

B. Their weapon belts. By laying your weapon belt at another man's feet you were saying to him, "I give you all my strength and military might. I will defend you to the death. Any enemy of yours is an enemy of mine. Furthermore, I will never use these weapons against you. I will not defend myself against you. For I lay myself completely open and defenseless before you."

C. Their names. Men would actually be known from that time forth by at least a part of the other man's name. The name denoted power of attorney. With the power of attorney to use a man's name, you can access his bank account and all his assets. What you say, he will back up. The right to use a man's name was and is very powerful.

D. Blood. Among non-Jewish peoples, the two covenanting friends would usually exchange their own blood in some fashion such as Dr. Trumbull described earlier. God forbade the Jewish people from drinking any blood because He did not want them partaking of the very life of another being. He knew that the life of the flesh is in the blood (Leviticus 17:14). Jesus, in John, chapter 6, spoke of this very thing as He commanded His followers to eat His flesh and drink His blood in order to receive His very life. This, of course, is what we are doing each time we partake of the Lord's Supper.

The Jews, however, did not drink or commingle each other's blood when they made covenant. They more frequently slew an animal and conducted their ceremony using the common blood of animals. This is the methodology we see used as God cut a covenant with Abraham in Genesis, chapter 15. The significance of blood being shed is that it is indicative of the life of the one cutting covenant. When a man sheds his own blood, or in the case of the Jews, the blood of a substitute, he is saying to the other party, "I am willing to give my life for you. I want to unite myself so closely with you that I actually want to be one with you by partaking of the very essence of your being and have your life inside me."

4. Vows: Men would make sacred vows to one another and to God. They would vow fidelity to one another unto death. They frequently would pronounce blessings to be bestowed upon their covenant partner as a result of the covenant and curses upon him should he ever break the covenant. These vows, because they were unilateral vows made unto God, were considered very sacred and were thus never broken.

5. Witnesses: The covenant ceremony was almost always attended by witnesses, who joyfully attested to the making of the covenant. There was frequently appointed a covenant attorney whose job it was to see that the covenant was carried out. Unlike our system of contract today, in which each party engages an attorney to protect his/her interests, under a covenant, there is only one attorney who is not for either party, but rather is a witness of the

covenant and is only for the covenant. It is his job to see to it that the vows and terms of the covenant are carried out.

6. Exchange of phylacteries: A phylactery is another word for a token of the covenant. Many times when men would cut a vein in the arm or leg and exchange blood, they would then pour gun powder or some such substance into the wound so as to create a noticeable black mark or scar which would serve to identify them as covenant men. Sometimes a copy of the document recording the covenant was worn in some sort of container by both parties on the arm, forehead or around the neck as an amulet. The phylactery was a sign to all that this person had entered into a blood covenant with another party. This is what God instructed the Jewish people to do when He made a covenant with them through Moses (Exodus 13:16).

7. Sharing of a covenant meal: After men would make a covenant together, as a symbol of their friendship, they would then sit and break bread together in hospitality and friendship.

The reason I have spent the time here to look at these components of a covenant is because most of us, as westerners, are not familiar with these things, because they are no longer a regular part of our culture. However, the entire Bible is a book of covenants. It is not a history book or story book. It is a book of covenants. We have been examining a basic value: Is marriage a covenant or is it a contract. It is interesting to me to note that even though most people do not understand covenant in the West at this time, our wedding ceremonies are still structured, for the most part, as though a marriage were a covenant. Obviously, the men who wrote the traditional wedding ceremony, still used in many contemporary churches, viewed marriage as a covenant. Let's look at the traditional wedding ceremony.

All the components of a blood covenant are inherent in the wedding ceremony.

1. Unilateral commitment before God: The ceremony is conducted in the presence of God, and unilateral promises are usually made to Him. The ceremony opens with words such as, "We are gathered here today **in the presence of God** and these witnesses to unite this man and this woman in **Holy Matrimony**, which is an honorable estate, instituted by God signifying unto us the mystical union that is between Christ and His Church."

2. Terms expressed: Terms are then expressed such as, "I take thee for better or for worse, for richer or for poorer, in sickness and in health, **until death do us part**." This again is a unilateral commitment before God of one partner to the other in whatever circumstance may arise until he/she dies.

3. Exchange of gifts: An exchange of gifts usually does occur. Hopefully the conveyance of the coat signifying standing and worth in each other's family is conveyed. Weapons are not usually conveyed, but hopefully each one makes him/herself open and vulnerable before the other. The groom usually does give the bride his name. Usually they do not exchange their own blood, however in many Christian churches, the marriage is sealed in communion by the substitutionary blood of Christ which was shed for both parties. Another symbol of the shedding of blood is the sexual union which usually occurs on the wedding night. This is another way of becoming one flesh, which is the purpose of the commingling of blood in a traditional blood covenant ceremony. The sexual union is meant to be a way of saying to the covenant partner, "I give you all that I am and all that I have, and I allow you access to the most precious and holy aspects of my being."

4. Vows: Vows are then pronounced in the ceremony. These vows are again quite unilateral and unconditional in most cases, such as, "I take thee to be my lawfully wedded Wife/Husband, to have and to hold from this day forward, for better or for worse, for richer or for poorer, in sickness and in health, to love and to cherish, until death do us part, according to God's holy ordinance, and thereto I pledge thee my troth."

5. Witnesses: Witnesses are also present who usually sign a marriage certificate. As a matter of fact, God Himself says that He is witness at a marriage. "*Because the Lord has been a witness between you and the wife of your youth, against which you have dealt treacherously, though she is your companion and your wife by covenant*" (Malachi 2:14).

6. Exchange of phylacteries: Phylacteries are then exchanged in the form of rings. These are received and then worn as an outward sign visible to all that this man or woman is in covenant.

7. Sharing of a covenant meal: A covenant meal is oftentimes held at the reception or rehearsal dinner. The weding cake is actually symbolic of the covenant meal, and many times the bride and groom serve this cake to each other in a special way to symbolize their unity and commitment to one another.

Let's now review the definition of a covenant: **A covenant is a unilateral, irrevocable, indissoluble commitment before God which is valid at least until death. A covenant is not dependent upon the choices of another, but is a commitment unto death before God.**

Let's now contrast this with the concept of a contract, which is an entirely different idea. **A contract is a bilateral agreement between two parties, totally dependent upon performance of the agreement, and breakable by either party upon non-performance of the other.** Under a contract, if one party fails to perform according to the contract, the other party has no obligation to perform either and is no longer bound by the terms of the contract.

As I mentioned earlier, I believe that we have experienced a major value exchange over the last fifty years of covenant for contract in marriage. Most people 50 years ago would have held a value that marriage is a covenant. I would suspect that most people today in western society would hold a value that marriage is a contract. However, we still use covenant language and pretend as though we think it is a covenant at wedding ceremonies.

I believe that in marriage this exchange of the value of covenant for the value of contract is responsible for a major portion of the abuse and dysfunction currently taking place in families. Let me explain. The covenant value in marriage would say to the marriage partner, "I am irrevocably committed to you until death separates us. My commitment to you has nothing to do with your performance or any choice you make. It is a unilateral commitment before God unto death." This is the commitment that Jesus made to us. *"I will never leave you or forsake you"* (Hebrews 13:5).

The contract value would rather say, "I'll keep my end of the bargain if you keep yours. If you make me unhappy or don't do what you promised, then I will leave you and find someone else who makes me happy and keeps his/her promises. And if you leave me, then I will definitely leave you and find someone else." **Aren't you glad that your relationship with Jesus is a covenant commitment on His part rather than a contract commitment?**

The result of this value exchange in my opinion has been devastating to the state of the family and of society. We now have a generation of people growing up who have no sense of permanency in anything. Everything is temporary, and there is no stability to life. You tell such people that God is stable and that His Word says that He never changes, and they cannot believe it. We have a generation of youth who cannot commit to anything. They have no ability to think long-term, so they simply make devastating short-sighted choices for themselves and their families as they marry. We have taken those things which are meant to be holy and desecrated them, making them common, and thereby stripped them of their value. Only that which is rare and special has value. That which is common is ordinary and carries no value. Covenant commitment is meant to protect the heart from damage. As we have forsaken the value of covenant in marriage, many have exposed their hearts to pressures and pain that God never intended for anyone's heart to experience. Because of this pain and deep wounding, pain avoidance has become the major value and driving force of many people's lives.

Some of the critical value questions which you need to decide are: Is your marriage a covenant before God or is it a contract? As you search the scriptures, do you find that the value of marriage presented in the Bible is that of covenant or that of contract? To what did you commit in your wedding? Did you commit before God to your husband/wife until death do us part? Are you a reactive puppet controlled by the words and behavior of your spouse and others, or are you a Spirit-led person, free to honor a commitment to God and your spouse, whether he/she does or not?

In review, we have talked in this chapter about three critical values which must be examined before we can construct a workable strategy for dealing with your spouse and your present circumstance. These are: 1) Do you value the Bible as God's Word and hold it to be definitive and authoritative in your life? 2) Are you committed to a self-sacrificial or a self-gratifying lifestyle? 3) Do you believe that marriage is a covenant or a contract? Again, the strategy you will construct for your future very much depends upon the values you hold.

---

[1]*For Further Reading*
McDowell, Josh. *Evidence That Demands a Verdict*. Campus Crusade for Christ, 1972
Bruce, F. F. *The New Testament Documents: Are They Reliable?* Chicago: Inter-Varsity Press, 1960
Little, Paul E. *Know What You Believe*, Wheaton: Scripture Press Publications, 1970
Pinnock, Clark H. *Set Forth Your Case*, Chicago: Moody Press, 1971
[2]Trumbull, H. Clay, *The Blood Covenant*, Kirkwood, Mo. Impact Books, Inc., 1975, pp.5-6
[3]Trumbull, H. Clay, *ibid*. p.7

Chapter 3

Biblical Perspective of Divorce & Remarriage

In the last chapter, we talked about the value of covenant in marriage vs. the value of contract. Embracing the value of covenant in marriage is not meant to be restrictive, but is rather meant to be protective. Let us now examine some of the consequences of abandoning the value of covenant in marriage. What is covenant meant to protect?

I believe that a covenant is meant to protect several things. It certainly protects the hearts of the two people involved. It can be very damaging to give your heart in romantic love to another person without the protection of a life-long commitment. A covenant in marriage creates a secure environment in which children can grow up. As important as these things are, I believe that the most important thing that **a covenant is meant to protect is the image of God in the sight of other people**. People's perception of the image of God is what determines whether they will accept Christ or not. I have noticed that when someone has a wrong image of God, even when the Gospel is clearly presented, such a person chooses death over life and refuses to receive Christ. It is extremely illogical that when presented with a clear choice of either eternal life or eternal death that a person would choose death. I have concluded that the primary reason for which someone makes such a choice is because he has a distorted image of Who God is. How does this happen?

I believe that there are two primary institutions on the earth which bear the image of God. These are: 1) Marriage, and 2) The Church. These two institutions are meant to depict to children and the world around Who God is and what He is like. In His prayer for the Church recorded in John 17, Jesus prayed the following:

> "*...that they may be one, just as We are one; I in them, and Thou in Me, that they may be perfected in unity, that the world may know that Thou didst send Me, and didst love them even as Thou didst love Me*" (John 17:22b-23).

In the above passage, Jesus states two reasons why the Church must be one: 1) That the world may know that the Father sent Jesus, and: 2) That the world may know that the Father loves them. Conversely, when the Church is divided, it is a bold statement to the world around us that the Father did not send Jesus and that the Father does not love people.

Jesus' concern in this passage is not only for the Church, but even more so for others before whom the Church is a representation of the image of God. No one individual is the representation of the image of God, but rather it is the collective relationship between believers that bears the image of God. When the Church is not one, it is difficult to convince people that the Father loves them and that He sent Jesus Christ.

Marriage Bears the Image of God

In the same way as the Church bears the image of God, so does marriage. Marriage was not man's idea, but rather is an institution of God. Apostle Paul tells us in Ephesians, chapter 5:22-33 that the relationship of Christ and the Church is depicted on earth by the relationship of a husband and wife. ***"'For this cause a man shall leave his father and mother, and shall cleave to his wife; and the two shall become one flesh.' This mystery is great; but I am speaking with reference to Christ and the Church"*** **(Ephesians 5:31-32).**

The traditional wedding ceremony begins with the statement, "We are gathered here today in the presence of God and these witnesses to unite this man and this woman in Holy Matrimony, which is an honorable estate, instituted by God, **signifying the mystical union that is between Christ and His Church.**" This means that if I want to find out how Jesus relates to me, I ought to look at the relationship between a man and his wife. If, when doing so, the primary value I see represented is the value of covenant, then I would be receiving a correct picture of Jesus' relationship to me. This covenant value would say, in the face of adversity, "I am irrevocably committed to you until death separates us. My commitment to you has nothing to do with your behavior or any choice you make. It is a unilateral commitment before God unto death." This, of course, is the commitment that Jesus has made to us as believers. ***"I will never leave you or forsake you"*** **(Hebrews 13:5).**

However, if, when looking to a marriage, the primary value I see represented is that of contract, then a wrong image of my relationship with Jesus is established in my heart. The contract value would rather say, "I'll keep my end of the bargain if you keep yours. If you make me unhappy or don't do what you promised, then I will leave you and find someone else who makes me happy and keeps his/her promises. And if you leave me, then I will definitely leave you and find someone else." I don't believe that this image is necessarily established through a conscious thinking process, but the heart naturally embraces the modeling of parents and other significant role models.

It is an even more serious situation when there is no distinction between the values of those called by the name of Christ (Christians) and unbelievers. If believers who ought to represent the values of God embrace the same values as society around them, then there is nowhere to look for a correct picture of relationship. Obviously, the primary impact upon the heart of a child comes through the relationship of his own parents. When a child looks at his parents and sees the value of contract presented in their marriage, it tends to release a tremendous fear of abandonment in the heart of the child. Why?

If the message presented between the parents is that of contract, "If you make me unhappy or don't measure up, I'm going to leave you and find somebody else," the heart of the child thinks, "I wonder what will happen to me if I make him/her unhappy and don't measure up?" In the heart, this feeling is naturally next transferred to God. Even as Paul said, the marriage is a picture of my relationship with Christ. In my relationship with Jesus, the heart conclusion is that I am like my mother, and Jesus is like my father. If I make Him unhappy, or don't do what is right, or leave Him, or am unfaithful to Him in any way, He is going to leave me and find someone else.

This creates a tremendous fear of abandonment even in relationship with God and results in an intense performance orientation and perfectionism in life. "I had better do everything just right and never sin, or Jesus will leave me and find someone else who does things right." Perfectionism and performance orientation are then the root of shame of self and others which results in family dysfunction and abuse. Dr. Sandra Wilson has written an excellent book, describing in detail this above mentioned process.

I highly recommend Dr. Wilson's book entitled, *Released From Shame, Recovery For Adult Children of Dysfunctional Families*.[1]

When Christian parents exchange the value of covenant for contract by embracing the practice of divorce or remarriage as a viable option for Christians, they open the door of their childrens' lives to the enemy and frequently release a literal generational curse. Through the above mentioned process a second generation is set up for family dysfunction in adulthood, frequently leading to divorce, thereby setting up the third generation for the same. This process then continues indefinitely until someone obtains knowledge of the process and chooses to break the cycle.

"*For lack of knowledge my people perish*" (Hosea 4:6).

Whether they realize it or not, parents hold in their hands a powerful key to the future lives of their children. Parents are the primary agents through whom impartation of image comes to children, either from God or from Satan. The image that I receive in my heart as a child about who I am, Who God is and how I relate to Him and others, often structures the course of my adult life. I believe that this is why Satan hates marriage so much. It is an earthly representation of the image of God and has primary impact upon generations of people. If Satan can get both partners to abandon covenant in marriage and become covenant breakers, then he can sow the wrong image of God into the hearts of the children and others looking on, thereby securing his ability to govern another generation and repeat in their lives many of the same destructive patterns.

As I mentioned earlier, in Ephesians, chapter 5, Apostle Paul tells us that the marriage relationship is an earthly picture of the relationship between Christ and the Church. When there is covenant keeping within a marriage, the image of Christ and His bride is correctly presented before children and the world around.

However, when there is covenant breaking within a marriage, the world is presented with the wrong earthly picture of Christ and His bride.

Because marriage does indeed bear the image of God in the world, just as Jesus stated in John 17 regarding the Church, as pertains to marriage, **both divorce and remarriage are bold statements to those around that the Father does not love them and that the Father did not send Jesus.** I have proven this out in practical experience when attempting to minister to the children of divorced and/or remarried couples. It is very difficult to convince these children that they are truly loved by God and that He really has sent Jesus to die for them. Often, deep inside, are feelings of unworthiness, shame, and a need to behave perfectly in order to receive God's love and acceptance. They have great difficulty believing that Jesus Christ is committed to love and accept them according to His covenant with them, independent of their behavior. They have never seen modeled covenant commitment independent of behavior. Through the selfishness of parents, Satan has, in such children, effectively set up the next generation to experience the same, if not worse, trauma and devastation in their own lives and families.

On the other hand, one of the most powerful presentations of the Gospel is when a marriage partner decides to uphold the value of covenant in marriage and remain a covenant keeper even in the face of unfaithfulness, or divorce, by a covenant breaking spouse. **Faithfulness in the sight of unfaithfulness is the message of the Gospel.** Jesus is faithful to His bride even when she is not faithful to Him. He never abandons her and looks for someone else. Thus covenant commitment protects the image of God in the sight of others and contributes to the expansion rather than the deterioration of the Kingdom of God on the earth. For more on this topic, see my book, *Marriage: Covenant or Contract*.

Jesus' Higher Standard

Believing that the Bible is authoritative and foundational to life, let's now look at what the Bible says regarding marriage, divorce, and remarriage. We will start in Matthew, chapter 5, verses 31 and 32. In this chapter, commonly known as the Sermon on the Mount, Jesus is contrasting the Old Covenant teaching of the Law with His New Covenant teaching. He prefaces this contrast with verse 17, in which he states, "*Do not think that I came to abolish the Law or the Prophets; I did not come to abolish, but to fulfill.*" He then goes on to contrast the many teachings by saying, "*You have heard that it was said* (the Pharisees' interpretation of the Law), *but I say to you* (Jesus' New Covenant teaching)." In all of these many contrasts in Matthew 5, Jesus quotes the Law and then establishes a stricter standard encompassing not only external behavior, but also inner attitudes of the heart.

You have heard it said:	**But I say unto you:**
Murder is sin.	Hatred in your heart is sin.
Adultery is sin.	Lust in your heart is sin.
If you divorce your wife, at least do it fairly with a certificate.	Divorce causes a wife to commit adultery, and to remarry a divorced woman is adultery (sin).
Do not make a false vow.	Do not vow at all. Just speak the truth.

Just retribution is fair when harmed or treated unjustly.	Do not even defend yourself or your possessions against injustice and evil.
Love your neighbor and hate your enemy.	Love your enemies and pray for those who persecute you.

The above is a summary of Jesus' contrast between the Pharisees' interpretation of the Old Covenant Law and Jesus' explanation of God's true intent of the Law. The Pharisees, using the letter of the Law, continually nullified God's intent behind the Law, so as to justify themselves as righteous keepers of the Law, and condemn others as unrighteous violators of the Law. In each statement above, Jesus exposes the perverted legalistic interpretation of the Law, and then reveals the true heart of the Father, for believers to deal with impure heart attitudes and to extend to those who sin against them God's forgiveness, grace, mercy, and love. The Pharisees did not deal with heart attitudes in their consideration of divorce and remarriage. But here Jesus suggests that a believer extend to a spouse sinning against him/her forgiveness, grace, and mercy, rather than tacitly applying the religious legalists' rules of justice and vindication through divorce and remarriage.

Let's look now at the specific words of Jesus in Matthew 5:31-32.

> *"And it was said, 'Whoever sends his wife away, let him give her a certificate of divorce;' but I say to you that everyone who divorces his wife except for the cause of unchastity* ***makes her commit adultery;*** *and whoever marries a divorced woman commits adultery"*
> (Matthew 5:31-32).

Jesus apparently assumes that in most situations in that culture a wife who has been put away by a husband will be drawn into a second marriage. Nevertheless, in spite of these pressures, He calls this second marriage adultery. The remarkable thing about the first half of Jesus' statement is that He applies this not only to a wife who is guilty of unchastity, but **He plainly states that the remarriage of a wife who, while innocent, has been divorced, is nevertheless adultery**. "*Everyone who divorces his wife except for the cause of unchastity makes* ***her (the innocent wife who has not been unchaste)*** *commit adultery*." I would assume that since an innocent wife who is divorced commits adultery when she remarries, that a guilty wife who remarries after divorce is all the more guilty. In the second part of the passage, Jesus plainly states that for anyone to marry a divorced woman, that person commits adultery.

In verse 32 of this passage, Jesus uses a phrase, "except for the cause of unchastity," which we are not going to deal with at this point. He uses the same phrase again in Matthew 19, and we will deal with the possible meanings of this phrase when we look at that passage. In summary, there are two very clear statements which Jesus makes in this Matthew 5 passage pertinent to our lives.

1. V. 32. A wife who is wrongly divorced, for a cause other than her unchastity, is not free to remarry another, but rather commits the sin of adultery when she remarries another person.

2. V. 32. Any man who marries a woman divorced from another man, commits the sin of adultery.

Jesus' Further Teaching on Divorce and Remarriage

Let us now move on and look at the passage in Matthew 19:3-12.

> *"And some Pharisees came to Him, testing Him, and saying, 'Is it lawful for a man to divorce his wife for any cause at all?' And He answered and said, 'Have you not read, that He who created them from the beginning*

> *made them male and female, and said, 'For this cause a man shall leave his father and mother, and shall cleave to his wife; and the two shall become one flesh'? 'Consequently they are no longer two, but one flesh. What therefore God has joined together, let no man separate.' They said to Him, 'Why then did Moses command to give her a certificate of divorce and send her away?' He said to them, 'Because of your hardness of heart, Moses permitted you to divorce your wives; but from the beginning it has not been this way.* ***And I say to you, whoever divorces his wife except for immorality, and marries another woman commits adultery.*** *The disciples said to Him, 'If the relationship of the man with his wife is like this, it is better not to marry.' But He said to them, 'Not all men can accept this statement, but only those to whom it has been given. For there are eunuchs who were born that way from their mother's womb; and there are eunuchs who were made eunuchs by men; and there are also eunuchs who made themselves eunuchs for the sake of the kingdom of heaven. He who is able to accept this, let him accept it'"*(Matthew 19:3-12).

It is important, in this case, to understand the context into which Jesus is speaking. There was a great controversy in those days among Jewish religious leaders between those who followed the teachings of Rabbi Shammai and those who followed Rabbi Hillel. The Pharisees are attempting, in this passage, to trap Jesus between the two schools of thought. Alfred Edersheim, a biblical scholar of the last century, in his insightful book, *Sketches of Jewish Social Life in the Days of Christ*, describes this controversy and the wisdom of Jesus in His answer.

"The fatal ease with which divorce could be obtained, and its frequency, appear from the question addressed to Christ by the Pharisees: 'Is it lawful for a man to put away his wife for every cause?' (Matt. xix. 3), and still more from the astonishment with which the disciples had listened to the reply of the Savior (ver.10). That answer was much wider in its range than our Lord's initial teaching in the Sermon on the Mount (Matt. v.32). To the latter no Jew could have had any objection, even though its morality would have seemed elevated beyond their highest standard, represented in this case by the school of Shammai, while that of Hillel, and still more Rabbi Akiba, presented the lowest opposite extreme. But in reply to the Pharisees, our Lord placed the whole question on grounds which even the strictest Shammaite would have refused to adopt. For the farthest limit to which he would have gone would have been to restrict the cause of divorce to 'a matter of uncleanness' (Deut. xxiv. 1), by which he would probably have understood not only a breach of the marriage vow, but of the laws and customs of the land. In fact, we know that it included every kind of impropriety, such as going about with loose hair, spinning in the street, familiarly talking with men, ill-treating her husband's parents in his presence, brawling, that is, 'speaking to her husband so loudly that the neighbours could hear her in the adjoining house' (Chehtub. vii. 6), a general bad reputation, or the discovery of fraud before marriage."[2]

When confronted in Matthew 19 by the Pharisees about what were the true legitimate grounds for divorce (the Pharisees having a very strict interpretation and the Saducees having a very liberal one), Jesus, in typical fashion, astounds them all, including His own disciples, by not picking either side. He instead refers them back to Genesis 2:24 and asserts that since God was the founder of marriage, there is no legitimate basis upon which man should attempt to dissolve a lawful marriage. "*What therefore God has joined together let no man separate.*"

The Pharisees then appeal to Moses' Law. Jesus acknowledges that the reason there was a provision made for divorce under the Old Covenant was not because it was right, or because God sanctioned it, but rather because people were so hard hearted that they were actually doing such a thing. So a provision was made to attempt to limit the extent of the damage. Jesus then again reveals God's heart of grace and forgiveness in relationship. Rather than agreeing with the legalistic approach of either the Pharisees or Saducees, who had specific rules by which it was permissible to divorce a wife, Jesus again calls His disciples to embrace God's heart and intent behind the commandment, saying that grace and forgiveness must be extended to an errant spouse. Thus, a man who under the laws of the religious leaders, would divorce his wife and marry another, according to Jesus, commits the sin of adultery.

From Jesus' perspective, the Pharisees were asking Him an utterly ridiculous question, basically, "Whose rules are applicable regarding divorce, Shammai's or Hillel's?" Jesus' answer is, "Nobody's. This ought not to be going on at all!" The Pharisees are really asking, "On what basis is it OK to commit adultery;" or "What are the rules by which we can do that which is wrong?" This would be like someone asking today, " If a man breaks into another man's house and steals his television, should the thief then, when caught, pay back the used or replacement value of the television?" Jesus would answer, "What? A man ought not to break into another man's home at all and steal his television. Have you not read that God said 'You shall not steal?'" The Pharisees then say, "Yes, but the laws of the State of Colorado say that if a man steals a TV he should pay back replacement value." Jesus would then say, "Yes, the law has a provision for stealing, not because it is right, but because people's hearts are so hard that they actually do such things, but this is not God's idea. And I say unto you that a man ought not to break into another man's house at all, and whoever does such a thing commits thievery."

Some modern-day Pharisees would then say, "But the man who stole the TV was not yet born again when he did so. He has since become a new creation in Christ and thus is now forgiven and absolved of all responsibility for his prior choices." This thought, of course, is so ludicrous that it is almost not worth a comment. I will, however, go ahead and state the obvious. It is wonderful that the former thief has become a Christian. Forgiveness, however, is predicated upon repentance, and restitution must still be made. In short, the former thief does not get to keep the TV just because he has become a Christian and now alleges that he has quit stealing. Biblical repentance and restitution require that he return the stolen TV and to the extent possible, make right what he has done wrong.

In verse 12, Jesus' disciples are obviously shocked by His statements. They recognize that Jesus is expressing God's covenant value of marriage as opposed to the contract value which most of the Jewish religious leaders held. They simply had different contracts. The disciples expressed to Jesus in verse 12 that if marriage were such a serious commitment as He had just described that perhaps it would be better not to marry. Jesus' covenant view of marriage was such a stark contrast to any of the views of the Jewish leaders, that even the disciples were shocked.

So far we can see five clear statements which Jesus makes in this Matthew 19 passage.

1. V. 4. It was God who created people; both male and female.

2. V. 5. God's purpose in creating both male and female was that they would leave their parents and join together in marriage as one flesh.

3. V. 6. Man's institution of divorce should never be allowed to separate people united by God's institution of marriage.

4. V. 8. Divorce under Moses was a concession of man to hard heartedness, but it is not and never has been God's idea.

5. V. 9. Any man who divorces his wife for any cause other than her unchastity and then remarries another woman commits the sin of adultery.

Some would argue that even though they are married, God did not join them together, therefore it is legitimate for them to be divorced. However, even when a couple does not know God when they marry, or may marry for entirely wrong motives, they have still chosen God's institution of marriage and I believe God was a witness to their marriage covenant. In Malachi 2:13-14, the Lord declares:

> *"And this is another thing you do; you cover the altar of the Lord with tears, with weeping and with groaning, because He no longer regards the offering or accepts it with favor from your hand. Yet you say, 'For what reason?'* ***Because the Lord has been a witness between you and the wife of your youth,*** *against whom you have dealt treacherously, though she is your companion and* ***your wife by covenant****" (Malachi 2:13-14).*

Except for the Cause of Unchastity

Let us now turn our attention to the phrase Jesus uses in Matthew 5:32 and Matthew 19:9, "except for the cause of unchastity." Several different views of the meaning of this scripture have been taken throughout history. These views are explained in much more detail in an excellent book entitled *Meant to Last*, written by Paul Steele and Charles Ryrie (of the Ryrie Study Bible).[3] For a much more detailed explanation of these matters, I highly recommend this book to you. However, at this point, I will give you a brief summary of some of the views which have been taken by Christians. It should be noted that some of these views are little heard of today outside of the circles of scholars and theologians, while others have received much more attention as a result of popular Christian books written for the general public. However, **the popularity of a view is not a particularly valid criterion for determining its accuracy.**

One view, referred to as the **Patristic View,** holds that the phrase "except for unchastity" means sexual immorality, namely adultery, during the course of the marriage. This view holds that when one partner has committed adultery, the non-adulterous partner may divorce the adulterous partner. If the non-adulterous partner does choose divorce, remarriage to another is not an option.

A second view, referred to as the **Betrothal View**, holds that Jesus' exception clause is talking about sexual immorality only during the betrothal period before the actual wedding took place. At the time of Christ, among the Jews, a betrothal (engagement) was just as binding as the actual marriage. If, on the wedding night, a man found that the woman he had married was not a virgin, he had a right to appeal to the local Sanhedrin the next day and have the marriage annulled. Alfred Edersheim states in his book, "*From the moment of her betrothal a woman was treated as if she were actually married. The union could not be dissolved, except by regular divorce; breach of faithfulness was regarded as adultery; and the property of the woman became virtually that of her betrothed, unless he expressly renounced it.*"[4]

We see Joseph seeking to divorce his engaged fiancee, Mary, when he found that she was pregnant (Matt. 1:18-19). This was the common remedy at the time for immorality committed during the time of engagement, before the actual wedding. The betrothal view holds that Jesus could not have been talking about adultery committed during the course of the marriage because of the Greek word used for unchastity. In both Matt. 5:32 and Matt. 19:9, the

Greek word used is *Porneia*, which is generally translated as fornication. It is distinguished from the Greek word for adultery which is *Moicheia*. The statement Jesus makes then in Matthew 19 is "Whoever divorces his wife, except for *porneia* (fornication), and marries another woman commits *moicheia* (adultery)."

The point is that the generally recognized remedy for adultery (immorality after the wedding) was stoning to death. If a wife had committed adultery, she would have been stoned to death and thus unavailable to be divorced by her husband. Obviously, Jesus' exception clause is not referring to adultery during the course of the marriage, but rather is referring to immorality committed during the betrothal period, which is why He used the word for fornication rather than the word for adultery.

The Betrothal view then holds that divorce is not permitted for those who are already married. Since divorce is not permitted, obviously remarriage is adultery. Jesus' only exception was for those who had committed fornication during the betrothal period. The engagement then had to be broken by a certificate of divorce, and this then is what Jesus was referring to when He said "except for fornication."

A third view, referred to as the **Consanguinity view** holds that Jesus' use of the word *Porneia* is specifically referring to the prohibited marriages between close blood relatives spoken of in Leviticus 18:6-18. Thus if a man had married his sister or mother, this is not a legitimate marriage and should be dissolved by divorce. This view holds that outside of homosexual marriage or marriage to a close blood relative, neither divorce nor remarriage is legitimate.

A fourth view promoted by Augustine, called the **Perteritive view** holds that Jesus' exception clause was a preterition, or a setting aside of the Shammai/Hillel controversy. I will not spend much time explaining this view as it is based on quite complicated exegesis of the text, which makes it lengthy and difficult to explain to English readers. This view holds that Jesus was saying, "I'm not going to comment on the meaning of *porneia* (fornication), but I will simply say that whoever divorces his wife and marries another woman commits adultery." Jesus then later, when alone with His disciples, clarified the issue to them in Mark 10:11. This view acknowledges that divorce sometimes happens, that it is not God's will and that remarriage is not an option.

The common thread running through all four of the above stated views is that they all strongly hold the value that marriage is a covenant before God. The legitimate reasons for divorce as held by these above mentioned views can be summarized as follows: 1. Adultery during marriage. 2. Discovery of fornication during the betrothal period. 3. Homosexual marriage or marriage to a close blood relative. The one tenet all four of these views have in common is that no matter what the reason for divorce might be, remarriage to another person is not an option for a follower of Jesus Christ. This, of course, is consistent with a covenant view of marriage.

Steele and Ryrie, in their book, *Meant to Last* state that the views of marriage of the early Church Fathers were that of covenant and were quite consistent up until the sixteenth century.

"Careful research through the hundreds of manuscripts written by church leaders of the first five centuries has revealed that with only one exception (Ambrosiaster, a fourth-century Latin writer), the Church Fathers were unanimous in their understanding that Christ and Paul taught that if one were to suffer the misfortune of divorce, remarriage was not permitted, regardless of the cause.[5]

This remained the standard view of the Church until the sixteenth century when Erasmus suggested a different idea that was taken over by Protestant theologians." [6, 7]

As mentioned above, a fifth view of marriage called the **Erasmian view** was concocted in the sixteenth century and promoted among the reformers by a classical humanist named Desiderius Erasmus. Erasmus did not hold a covenant view of marriage but rather held that of contract. Without realizing it, many of the protestant reformers exchanged the former value of covenant in marriage for that of contract in embracing some of Erasmus's thinking. Steele and Ryrie write of Erasmus:

"Erasmus, a contemporary of Martin Luther, was considered a friend of the Reformation because he spoke out against the abuses of power of the Catholic Church. Luther broke with him, however, because of Erasmus's heretical ideas and his weak view on justification by faith. But for some reason, Luther favored his ideas on divorce and remarriage, thus rejecting the teaching and practice of the early church."[8]

"It is curious that though Erasmus was essentially regarded as a heretic by his contemporaries, the Reformation writers were greatly influenced by his doctrine of divorce and remarriage. Since most evangelical literature has in turn been influenced by the reformers and subsequently by the Westminster Confession, his view is widely held among evangelicals today."[9]

The Erasmian view holds that Jesus' exception in Matthew 19 refers to adultery. The further assumption is that since according to the Old Covenant Law the adulterer is to be stoned to death, that under the New Covenant the adulterous party is not killed, but rather is "as dead in God's sight." The logic then goes that since the adulterous partner is as dead, the "innocent" partner is free to remarry. The Erasmian view allows for both divorce and remarriage of the "innocent" party in the cases of both adultery or desertion.

This viewpoint represents a complete exchange of the value of covenant for the value of contract in marriage and a significant departure from the viewpoint held by the Church Fathers up until the time of Erasmus. I believe that the Erasmian viewpoint is very difficult to support from Scripture and is rather more based upon the subjective feelings and opinions of those who support this view.

Those who hold the Erasmian viewpoint make a significant assumption that if I am not responsible for divorce or I have been forgiven for divorce, that I am somehow now free to remarry. This is actually just the opposite of what Jesus taught. He taught as we saw earlier in Matthew 5:32 that even an innocent wife who was wrongly divorced commits the sin of adultery if she remarries another person. Thus divorce and remarriage are two entirely separate sin issues. Not being responsible for or being forgiven for divorce does in no way authorize one to commit the further sin of adultery through remarriage.

This is no different than alleging that because a pregnant teenager was raped or has repented of the sin of fornication and has been forgiven by the blood of Jesus that she is now free to commit the sin of murder through aborting the baby. NO! Fornication and abortion are two separate sins as are divorce and remarriage. They are not linked together. Freedom from one does not authorize commission of the other. **If John The Baptist had heard and embraced Erasmus' teaching in his day, he would have lived to a ripe old age and would not have lost his head.**

After a much more extensive investigation of these five views, Steele and Ryrie bring the following summary with which I heartily agree.

"In summary, all five views presented here agree on some basic points.

- *God's best is monogamy and He hates divorce.*
- *Divorce under the law was a concession to hard hearts.*
- *Christ taught and upheld God's highest standard in His teaching.*

The Patristic view and the Erasmian view agree that Porneia may mean adultery. But the Erasmian view is the only one to allow remarriage after divorce. The other views, while recognizing that divorce may sometimes happen for various reasons, are unanimous in their conviction that remarriage is contrary to Scripture, and never permitted.

The eunuch saying in Matthew 19 indicates that Christ was not siding with either Hillel or Shammai but was presenting a concept revolutionary to the minds of the disciples. The Erasmian view ignores this context as irrelevant to what Christ said in the preceding verses. It also fails to explain adequately the clear teaching of Mark 10 and Luke 16, while the other four views see those texts as supporting their thesis that no remarriage is allowed. That also seems the most consistent with Paul's understanding of the meaning of Christ's words as given in 1 Corinthians 7:10-13.

The believer who suffers the misfortune of a divorce has two clear options: remain unmarried or be reconciled to one's mate. To teach anything else is inconsistent with God's standard for marriage."[10]

Further Teaching by Jesus

Let us now look at Jesus' teaching in Mark 10:2-12.

> *"And some Pharisees came up to Him, testing Him, and began to question Him whether it was lawful for a man to divorce a wife. And He answered and said to them, 'What did Moses command you?' And they said, 'Moses permitted a man to write a certificate of divorce and send her away.' But Jesus said to them, 'Because of your hardness of heart he wrote you this commandment. But from the beginning of creation God made them male and female. For this cause a man shall leave his father and mother, and the two shall become one flesh; consequently they are no longer two, but one flesh. What therefore God has joined together, let no man separate.' And in the house the disciples began questioning him about this again. And He said to them,* ***'Whoever***

> ***divorces his wife and marries another woman commits adultery against her; and if she herself divorces her husband and marries another man, she is committing adultery'"*** (Mark 10:2-12).

This passage is very similar to the one in Matthew 19. The primary difference is that no exception clause is included in this Mark 10 teaching. This passage is very clear and easy to understand. Some of the points which Jesus very clearly states in this passage are:

1. V. 9. What God has joined together let no man separate.
2. V. 11. Any man who divorces his wife and marries another woman commits the sin of adultery.
3. V. 12. Any woman who divorces her husband and marries another man commits adultery.

Let's look now at Jesus' teaching in Luke.

> ***"Everyone who divorces his wife and marries another commits adultery; and he who marries one who is divorced from a husband commits adultery"*** (Luke 16:18).

Again this passage is very clear and easy to understand. I don't know any other way to interpret this other than that everyone who divorces his wife and marries another person commits adultery; and whoever marries one who is divorced from a husband commits adultery. Jesus here clearly states:

1. Any man who divorces his wife and marries another commits the sin of adultery.
2. Any man who marries a woman divorced from another man commits the sin of adultery.

In examining the above passages it is important to determine whether Jesus' overall view of marriage is that of a unilateral covenant commitment unto death, or whether He views marriage as a bilateral contract breakable by either party, particularly if the one party defaults. The reason that this is important is because we obviously want to align our values with those of Jesus Christ. Because the Erasmian view of divorce and remarriage has become so widespread in protestant churches, many people approach the Bible with a preconceived value of marriage as a contract. There is thus an underlying assumption then that Jesus' exception in Matthew 5 and 19 refers to adultery, which is then called "scriptural grounds" for divorce and that remarriage is automatically permitted. Jesus actually states just the opposite in Matthew 5:32, that even the non-adulterous wife who is a victim of divorce commits the sin of adultery if she remarries another man.

If one were to lay aside all presuppositions and look at these passages as objectively as possible, it is very clear to me that the concept of marriage which Jesus embraced and was espousing was that of an irrevocable, unilateral covenant unto death, rather than that of a breakable contract. I believe that this is especially true in light of the fact that Apostle Paul tells us that marriage is the earthly picture of the relationship between Christ and His bride. I do not believe that Jesus would abandon any of us (His bride) because we were unfaithful to Him or deserted Him. As a matter of fact He states just the opposite in Hebrews 13:5, *"I will never desert you, nor will I ever forsake you."*

What About God's Grace?

Some Christians who have embraced an Erasmian view of divorce and remarriage react against the clear teaching of Scripture in this area, saying that to believe that the Bible means exactly what it says is legalistic, unloving and a violation of God's grace. Many such people believe that God's grace is God's permission to willfully sin and to continue sinning. I believe that this is just the opposite of the biblical concept of grace. I like to define grace as God's manifest power and presence enabling one to carry out God's will. Grace is not the right to do what you want, but rather the desire and power to do what is right.

Unfortunately, for most people, theology is dictated by morality. In other words, people first decide how they want to live and then go to the Bible to find texts which justify their worldview and lifestyle. Then those who hold a stricter interpretation than they do are called legalists and those who hold a looser interpretation are called compromisers. Of course the perfect standard by which all is weighed is how they see it.

Suppose we were to apply this same concept of grace and view of scripture to other controversial biblical issues such as homosexuality or abortion. This, of course, is exactly what the homosexual community would like to have the Church do, regarding their lifestyle and practices. They accuse us of hating them and shaming them because we say that homosexual practices are an abomination before God. The majority of the Church would contend that homosexual practices are indeed sin against God based on the clear teaching in Romans 1, Leviticus 18, and other biblical passages. Again, the teaching in Romans 1 is very clear and needs no interpretation other than what is clearly stated. Those who claim to be followers of Christ and embrace and practice homosexuality as a lifestyle, however, would accuse those who believe the Bible of being unloving, legalistic and of treating them as second class Christians.

I have met many such people who are practicing homosexuals and claim that they are born again and love the Lord. They have found ways to justify to themselves that their homosexual practice is not sin, but that their beliefs and practices are simply different than mine. They, therefore, accuse me of intolerance and violating Jesus' grace, mercy and forgiveness in the New Covenant if I continue to maintain that their practice is not just a matter of opinion, but is indeed sin. They say, "We respect your choice of sexual practices and don't call what you do an abomination before God. We even respect your choice not to participate, but why do you insist on calling what we do sin and an abomination to God?" Their concept of New Covenant grace and forgiveness tells them that because they believe in Jesus, they are free by God's grace to practice what they will, and the rest of the Church should receive their practices.

This same tactic is, of course, foisted upon us by those in the liberal church who believe that abortion is not sin and is simply the mother's choice. They continue to repeat this lie and insist that it is God's grace and mercy to those who were sexually promiscuous or have suffered the misfortune of being raped, for us as loving brothers and sisters to aid and support such a one as she aborts her baby.

What I am saying is that God's grace under the New Covenant is not an excuse to justify sin as right and then to continue willfully sinning and ask others in the Church to back off and not say that they are sinning; just keep their opinions to themselves so as not to shame those who are engaging in such practices. I do not believe that grace under the New Covenant is God's permission to continue sinning willfully. Apostle Paul said, "*For sin shall not be master over you, for you are not under law, but under grace. What then? Shall we sin because we are not under law but under grace? May it never be!*" (Romans 6:14-15). I believe that God's grace delivers us from sin and empowers us to discontinue sin.

I believe that we could liken the practice of divorce and remarriage to homosexuality, abortion, or any other area of sin. As believers, we are called to show love toward a practicing homosexual who says that he is born again and loves Jesus. I have no problem separating identity from behavior so that I can love him, extend to him God's grace and mercy, but I cannot say that his practice is not wrong. If he feels like a second class citizen or shamed by this I can only minister to him that what he is experiencing is not shame, which is based in wrongness of personhood, but is actually guilt which is based in wrongness of behavior because that which he is doing is in reality, before God, sin. Guilt is a good thing that God put in our lives to tell us that what we are doing is wrong. As long as one continues to justify a sinful practice as being right rather than agreeing with God and repenting and receiving forgiveness, one will never be free of guilt. If one truly believes before God that this practice is correct, then he will obviously mistake the true guilt of the sin as shame and thus never repent and therefore never be free of guilt.

Thus, in your present situation, God's grace to you is not His permission to go ahead and divorce your spouse, or remarry anyone else. God's grace is His manifest love, power and presence in your life, enabling you to stand firm with God against Satan for the restoration of your marriage.

Apostle Paul's Teaching on Marriage

Let us now look at Apostle Paul's teaching in I Corinthians 7. This entire chapter deals with marital relationships. We will look here only at the passages that deal with divorce and remarriage.

> *"But to the married I give instructions, not I, but the Lord, that the wife should not leave her husband* ***(but if she does leave, let her remain unmarried, or else be reconciled to her husband), and that the husband should not send his wife away.*** *But to the rest I say, not the Lord, that if any brother has a wife who is an unbeliever, and she consents to live with him, let him not send her away. And a woman who has an unbelieving*

> *husband, and he consents to live with her, let her not send her husband away. For the unbelieving husband is sanctified through his wife, and the unbelieving wife is sanctified through her believing husband; for otherwise your children are unclean, but now they are holy. Yet if the unbelieving one leaves, let him leave; the brother or the sister is not under bondage in such cases, but God has called us to peace. For how do you know, O wife, whether you will save your husband? Or how do you know, O husband, whether you will save your wife?"*
> I Corinthians 7:10-16.

The clear instruction which Apostle Paul gives here in verses 10 and 11 is that a wife is not to leave her husband. This could also be applied to the husband's leaving his wife. The clear teaching here is that if a spouse violates this teaching and does leave for some reason, the one who has left is not to remarry. There are two clear options given in verse 11: Either be reconciled with the spouse, or remain single. Again, remarriage to someone else is not an option. This is consistent with the covenant view of marriage held by Jesus.

Paul then addresses the issue of an unbelieving spouse. His instruction is that if the unbelieving spouse consents to live with the believer, let him/her do so. However, if the unbeliever is unwilling to continue the marriage relationship and wants to leave, the believer is not bound to attempt to force him/her to stay. Those who hold an Erasmian, contractual view of marriage naturally assume that there is an implied release in verse 15 for the remaining spouse to remarry.

This, however is only an assumption about an implication. This is not at all stated clearly. Actually, verse 16 would indicate just the opposite. Paul here asks the remaining spouse the question, "For how do you know, O wife/husband whether you will save your husband/wife?" This statement implies that faithfulness of the remaining spouse may be the key to the salvation of the departing spouse. This would definitely preclude the remarriage of the remaining spouse to someone else.

A second reason that it is highly unlikely that Paul is, in verse 15, implying that the remaining, believing spouse is free to remarry if the unbelieving spouse leaves, is because of his summary statement at the end of the chapter. After giving much instruction throughout the entire chapter, Paul concludes with a summary statement in verses 39 and 40 which clearly state the conditions for release from a spouse.

> "*A wife is bound as long as her husband lives; but if her husband is dead, she is free to be married to whom she wishes, only in the Lord. But in my opinion she is happier if she remains as she is; and I think that I also have the Spirit of God*" (I Corinthians 7:39-40).

Thus in his summary statement, Paul tells us that a wife is not free to remarry as long as her husband is living. I don't know any other way to interpret this other than that a wife is bound as long as her husband lives. If this is stated in his summary statement in verse 39 as it is, it would be ridiculous to think that he would contradict himself back in verse 15 by saying that a wife was free to remarry if her unbelieving husband left her. This summary statement confirms that the value which Apostle Paul held of marriage was that of unilateral covenant, not of contract.

The argument is made by some who hold the Erasmian view that Paul is speaking to divorced people in verses 27 and 28 and, as such, is telling them that they have not sinned if they marry, which, of course, would be a remarriage to someone other than their spouse.

> *"Are you bound to a wife? Do not seek to be released. Are you released from a wife? Do not seek a wife. But if you should marry, you have not sinned; and if a virgin should marry, she has not sinned. Yet such will have trouble in this life, and I am trying to spare you"* (I Corinthians 7:27-28).

The argument is that in verse 28 Paul is addressing two categories of people, **virgins** and **others**. He says, "If you should marry, you have not sinned;" He then addresses virgins. "You," then is obviously a different category than "virgins." It is clear that the "you" addressed in verse 28 is those who are spoken of in verse 27 as those who have been "released" from a wife. The assumption is that those who are released from a wife are divorced people. This is a totally erroneous assumption, as Paul clearly tells us in verse 39 that a wife is only released from her husband by his death, not by his divorce. Paul further confirms in Romans 7 how a wife is released from her husband.

> *"For the married woman is bound by law to her husband while he is living; but if her husband dies, she is released from the law concerning the husband. So then if, while her husband is living she is joined to another man, she shall be called an adulteress; but if her husband dies, she is free from the law, so that she is not an adulteress, though she is joined to another man* (Romans 7:2-3).

The obvious point is that those who are released from a spouse, according to Paul, are widowers and widows. Never once in I Corinthians 7 does Paul mention anything about divorced people marrying. He talks about two categories of marriageable people: widows and virgins. **Thus "those who have not sinned if they marry," spoken of in verse 28, are virgins and widows, not divorced people.**

God Hates Treachery in Marriage

Let us now look at a passage in Malachi in which God expresses His attitude toward both divorce and remarriage.

> *"And this is another thing you do: you cover the altar of the Lord with tears, with weeping and with groaning, because He no longer regards the offering or accepts it with favor from your hand. Yet you say, 'For what reason?' Because* ***the Lord has been a witness between you and the wife of your youth, against whom you have dealt treacherously,*** *though she is your companion and your wife by covenant. But not one has done so who has a remnant of the Spirit. And what did that one do while he was seeking a godly offering? Take heed then, to your spirit, and let no one deal treacherously against the wife of your youth.* ***'For I hate divorce,' says the Lord, the God of Israel,*** *'and him who covers his garment with wrong,' says the Lord of hosts. 'So take heed to your spirit, that you do not deal treacherously'"* (Malachi 2:13-16).

Malachi is most certainly describing a particular situation in this passage. Malachi was a contemporary of Ezra. He prophesied at the time of the reconstruction of the temple in Jerusalem under the direction of Ezra and Nehemiah. It is highly likely that the treachery against the young wives spoken of in Malachi 2 is described in Ezra chapter 10.

> *"And Shecaniah the son of Jehiel, one of the sons of Elam, answered and said to Ezra, 'We have been unfaithful to our God, and have married foreign women from the peoples of the land; yet now there is hope for*

> *Israel in spite of this. So now* ***let us make a covenant with our God to put away all the wives and their children,*** *according to the counsel of my lord and of those who tremble at the commandment of our God; and let it be done according to the law..."*
>
> *"Then Ezra the priest stood up and said to them, 'You have been unfaithful and have married foreign wives adding to the guilt of Israel. Now, therefore, make confession to the Lord God of your fathers, and do His will; and separate yourselves from the peoples of the land and from the foreign wives"* (Ezra 10:2-3; 10-11).

The situation was such that many of the men of Israel had divorced their Jewish wives and taken heathen wives from the nations around them. The Lord says in Malachi 2:14 that He was witness to the covenant made with the original Jewish wives. He calls the divorce of the original wives treachery and further states that He hates divorce. In verse 14 God speaks of the wife of their youth as being the wife by covenant. **God, then through Ezra commands all the men who have taken foreign wives to divorce them and send them away (Ezra 10:11).**

The issue with the marriages in Ezra was twofold. Firstly, the men had married women who worshipped idolatrous gods. God had forbidden the people of Israel from marrying such people. Secondly, it appears that the men had divorced their original wives in favor of these foreign wives. This, God calls treachery and says that He hates it. The point is that both divorce and remarriage to another person are acts of covenant breaking and are in and of themselves sins against God, which require repentance, forgiveness, and restitution. Abandonment of a legitimate marriage through divorce is an act of covenant breaking. Remarriage to another person by either party while the spouse is yet living, is equally an act of covenant breaking, and is sin.

---

[1]Dr. Sandra Wilson, *Released From Shame, Recovery For Adult Children of Dysfunctional Families* (Downers Grove, Ill.: Intervarsity Press, 1990.
[2]Edersheim, Alfred, *Sketches of Jewish Social Life in the Days of Christ*, Grand Rapids, Mich.: Wm. B. Erdmans Publishing Co., 1988, pp. 157-158.
[3]Paul E. Steele and Charles C. Ryrie, *Meant to Last*, Wheaton, Ill.: Victor Books, 1986.
[4]op. cit. Alfred Edersheim, p. 148.
[5]Gordon Wenham, *The Biblical Way of Marriage and Divorce, #3, New Testament Teaching*, Third Way (London), November 17, 1977.
[6]Bill Heth, *An Analysis and Critique of the Evangelical Protestant View of Divorce and Remarriage*, Th.M. Thesis, Dallas Theological Seminary, May 1982, p.8.
[7]op. cit. Paul E. Steele and Charles C. Ryrie, p.89.
[8]op.cit. Paul E. Steele and Charles C. Ryrie, p.104.
[9]ibid. , p. 90.
[10]ibid., p115.

Chapter 4

Building a Future Life Strategy

Let us now review the ground we have covered so far in this book. In chapter one we talked about allowing God to expose the faulty foundations in your life, and rebuild in you a life of strong internal character. We talked about making Jesus Christ the foundation of your life, getting free of idolatry toward your spouse, becoming a proactive rather than reactive person, and growing up emotionally into a state of interdependence rather than dependence or independence.

In chapter two we talked about principles, values and strategies. Strategies for living are based on the values one holds, which are based on one's understanding of life principles. In order for a strategy to be effective and successful, two things must be true: 1) it must be consistent with the inherent values of the one hoping to implement the strategy, and 2) the values underlying the strategy must be consistent with true life principles. Since most people have never thought through their values, we then examined three critical values, upon which we can now construct a successful strategy consistent with true life principles.

We first started with the simple value of how truth is determined. If you have no reliable method for determining true life principles, then you have no ability to know whether your values are in line with truth, reality and how life really works, or not. We determined that the Bible is God's source of true life principles and can be relied upon as a true basis of doctrine and conduct. The Bible is the inerrant Word of God and is definitive and authoritative in the life of a believer in Jesus Christ.

We next looked at the value of self-sacrifice vs. the value of selfishness. We came to see that self-sacrifice is an inherent biblical value which even most of the world naturally recognizes as a correct and virtuous value. Selfishness is universally rejected by all as wrong and destructive. To embrace self-sacrifice regarding marriage means that you are more concerned about the reputation and image of God in the sight of your children and others than you are about your own personal happiness and emotional well-being.

The final value which we examined is that of covenant vs. contract in marriage. We came to see that our relationship with God is not a contract, but rather is a covenant made by the blood of Jesus Christ. Likewise, a marriage is meant to be an earthly picture of Christ's relationship with His Church, and thus is meant to be a covenant and not a contract. To embrace the value of covenant in marriage is to acknowledge that marriage is a unilateral, life-long commitment, breakable only by death.

In chapter three we examined some of the consequences of abandoning the biblical value of covenant in marriage and exchanging it for the worldly value of contract. Having accepted the value that the Bible is the Word of God and is God's source of true life principles upon which correct values can be established, we then examined the Bible's teaching regarding marital relationships, divorce and remarriage.

Building a Strategy For Your Life

We are now ready to construct a strategy for dealing with your marital relationship based upon the previously discussed values. As I mentioned earlier, this strategy will be successful only if it is consistent with the values held by the person attempting to implement it. To attempt to implement a strategy reliant upon values which you really do not hold is doomed, for certain, to failure. This strategy is based upon a commitment to allow God to develop in you the strong, proactive character we spoke of in chapter one. It is also based upon the values of the authority of the Bible, self-sacrifice, and covenant in marriage. If you embrace these biblical values then this strategy is for you and has been found to be highly effective in bringing about marital reconciliation and healing for families.

If you are at the point in your marriage where either your spouse, you, or both want to leave the marriage, there are three basic strategies which could be pursued, but only one of them is based on the values about which we have spoken. You could: 1) Renounce your commitment to, and the Lordship of, Jesus Christ in your life, separate from and forget your spouse, "go on with your life" and seek a new partner or do whatever else you please. 2) Separate from your spouse, commit yourself to remain single and forget your spouse. 3) Recommit yourself to Jesus Christ and to your marriage, commit yourself to remain single if involuntarily separated or divorced, and exercise faith in God for the healing and restoration of your marriage.

Obviously option one is no option at all for those who love Jesus and to Whom He means more than life itself. This is the course of the reactive, committed to self-gratification, their own happiness, contract in marriage, to whom the Word of God carries no authority to govern their lives. The gospel of Mark records in chapter 5 Jesus' encounter with a severely demonized man. He was so severely deranged by the demons that he was even unable to live in society, but rather lived out among the tombs. The demons gave him such supernatural strength that he was able to break any chains and shackles with which people had tried to subdue him. This man was extremely tormented and totally crazy as a result of the demonization. Imagine if such a man were your spouse! (You may be thinking at this point, "It is! You have just given a pretty accurate description of my spouse.") When this man finally encountered Jesus, He cast the legion of demons out of the man and into a herd of swine, who immediately rushed down a hill and perished in the sea. The man was totally set free and begged Jesus to let him accompany Him. Jesus, however, did not let him, but rather instructed him to "*Go home to your family and report to them what great things the Lord has done for you, and how He had mercy on you*" (Mark 5:19).

Imagine if after this great deliverance, the man were to go home as Jesus instructed him, only to find that his wife was a covenant breaker, had abandoned him, divorced him and had remarried someone else. I have encountered many Christians who seem to have faith to believe God for the healing of cancer, but have no faith to believe God for the healing of a marriage.

Option two is a viable option, but I do not believe it is God's best, and does not embrace all of the above mentioned biblical values. As Apostle Paul stated regarding a spouse who has left, "*For how do you know O wife, whether you will save your husband? Or how do you know, O husband, whether you will save your wife?*" (I Corinthians 7:16). I believe that God oftentimes intends to use a faithful, believing spouse as a testimony to the errant spouse to eventually influence him/her to submit to Christ. I have spoken to many reunited couples in which exactly this has been the case.

Option three is to commit yourself to uphold your marriage as a unilateral covenant commitment before God, independent of your spouse's choices, rebuild faulty foundations in your own life, and exercise faith for a total transformation of yourself and your spouse. This total reconciliation and healing of your marriage is the strategy most consistent with the previously stated biblical values. You say, "That type of transformation and healing would take an absolute miracle from God." The point is, God is in the miracle business. My friend, Dave Duell, a strong visionary and mighty man of faith, is fond of saying, "Any vision which can be accomplished naturally and does not require faith and the supernatural intervention of God is not worthy to be called God's work or God's vision."

It is important at this point to remind you that the battle for your marriage is not a battle against flesh and blood, but rather is a spiritual battle against deceptive forces of wickedness in the heavenlies who have deceived your spouse and have sought to deceive you. Satan and the entire kingdom of darkness hate you, your marriage and especially God's image in the "one flesh" relationship of your marriage. To put it very simply, it is God's desire to heal you and your spouse and to restore your marriage as a testimony to His glory, while it is Satan's desire to destroy your marriage as a testimony to his glory. There is not really any neutral ground. Your choice is either to submit yourself to God's grace and God's plan or submit yourself to Satan's plan of destruction. I am not saying that you can control circumstances, but you can submit yourself to and set yourself in agreement with either God or Satan. You must decide either to take a bold stand with God for your marriage, against Satan, or to submit yourself to Satan for the destruction of your marriage. "*Submit therefore to God. Resist the devil and he will flee from you*" (James 4:7).

We will spend the rest of this chapter talking about implementing the third, above mentioned strategy of committing yourself to your marriage, rebuilding the faulty foundations of your life, and exercising faith for the transformation of yourself, your spouse, and the total restoration of your marriage. I will now give you seven practical steps in implementing this strategy.

STEP ONE

Affirm your commitment under the Lordship of Jesus Christ to remain single by God's grace until the death of your spouse or the restoration of your marriage. Affirm before God that remarriage to another person for you as a Christian would be adultery and is not an option. If you do not make a strong commitment to God at this point to remain faithful to your marriage covenant regardless of your spouse's choices, you will be tempted at many critical points in the battle to give up and find false comfort in letting your heart become wrongly attached in relationship to another person. Jesus must be made the center of your life. This strategy will be extremely difficult to implement and see through to the end if your primary concern is still for yourself, your emotional well being and not for the name and Kingdom of Jesus Christ. If you are at the point where your marriage is disintegrating or close to it, there has already been much emotional wounding, and there is already a lot of spiritual deception at work. When people are deeply wounded, they quickly move into pain avoidance and self-gratification mode, and, in deception, find ways to justify whatever short-term solutions they think will alleviate pain and bring a measure of comfort. This strategy requires a long-term commitment to a spiritual battle to overcome the deception of the forces of spiritual wickedness which have probably captured your spouse and are now seeking to destroy your marriage.

STEP TWO

Check the character and foundational values of your life which we examined in chapters 1 and 2. In order for this strategy to be effective, you must have relinquished your spouse from being the center of your life, renounced any idolatry towards him/her and made Jesus Christ the center of your life. You must have chosen to let God grow you up emotionally to make you an interdependent person, rather than an emotionally dependent or independent person. As a person committed to emotional growth and maturity, you must have chosen to become a proactive person rather than a reactive person. Your choices must be yours, because they are right and based on deeply held values, not simply reactions to the words and choices of others.

This strategy requires that you exchange the value of selfishness and self-gratification for that of self-sacrifice and living for a cause greater than yourself. You must also have exchanged society's value of bilateral contract in marriage for the biblical value of unilateral covenant in marriage. You must also recognize that this is not just a "technique by which you can fix your broken marriage," but rather it is the embracing of a lifestyle which you will live for the rest of your life. This is not really about your marriage. This is about the total surrender of your life to Jesus Christ.

You can know that God wants to heal your marriage far more than even you do, but if you think that embracing these values and committing yourself to this strategy will somehow win favor with God and help your marriage, you are still deceived, as you are in idolatry, trying to use God and/or biblical principles to accomplish your will rather than coming to the cross of Christ, dying to your will and living for His will. You see, this strategy functions only on the basis that life is not about your will but about God's will. This is the point. From this standpoint, you must see that the purpose of the healing of your marriage is for the glory of God and the upholding of His image and name in the sight of others, not for your personal pleasure and well-being. These are only the by-product, in which God takes great pleasure, but they are not the goal of this strategy.

STEP THREE

Relinquish your partner to God. Do not continue to try to hang on to him/her if he/she wants to leave. This is one of the most difficult concepts to get across to people. You must learn to commit yourself unconditionally to hold on to your marriage covenant and your faith in God's desire and ability to restore your marriage, but at the same time to let go of your spouse. Many people continue to try in the power of their own strength to hang on to their partners, doing anything so that the spouse will not leave. This actually delays the process that you, your spouse and marriage must go through in order to be healed by God.

Most of the time, that which is old must die in order for that which is new to become alive. Jesus stated that new wine cannot be poured into an old wineskin without bursting the skin. He also talked about a seed's needing to fall into the ground and die in order for it to germinate and bring forth new life. You don't need a modified form of your old marriage relationship. You need a resurrected marriage. The longer you try to control your spouse's choices, hold on to him/her and fix that which is severely broken, the more you delay the process of death and resurrection. Oftentimes in a broken marriage, both spouses need to undergo an entire transformation before they are fit to relate to one another again in a marital relationship.

STEP FOUR

Pray. As I mentioned several times before, the battle for your marriage is not against your spouse, but rather is against the forces of spiritual wickedness who hate God and your marriage, (Ephesians 6:10-12). You must learn how to conduct spiritual warfare on behalf of your spouse, yourself, your children, and your marriage. The choices your spouse may be making at this time are not simply his/her choices, but rather are strongly influenced by deception and delusion of the enemy. You cannot make another person's choices for him or her, but in prayer you certainly can impact the spiritual and emotional forces which work to establish ungodly strongholds and deceive your spouse.

It is critical for you to establish a strong regular daily prayer life. You must learn how to strengthen yourself and your family through prayer as well as how to intercede for your spouse.

STEP FIVE

Exercise faith in God for the transformation of your life, your spouse's life and the resurrection of your marriage. This strategy works only by faith in God's desire and ability to accomplish His will in your life and marriage. Apostle Paul tells us in Romans 10:17 that "*faith comes by hearing and hearing by the word of Christ.*" There are two words used in the Greek language which are translated in English as *word*. One word is *logos* and the other is *rhema*. Logos tends to mean the general Word of God written for all to read. Rhema, on the other hand, tends to mean the specific Word of God quickened by the Holy Spirit to a specific person, at a specific time, for a specific purpose.

In the matter of Goliath's challenging Israel in I Samuel 17, all, including Saul, probably knew the Word God had given to Israel that He would fight their battles and drive the enemies out of the land before them. This was a general word (logos in Greek) to all Israel. However, only David had a revelation from God (rhema) which gave him the confidence to actually slay the Philistine giant. This revelation of the Word of the Lord gave David such a confidence and boldness that he was able to convince Saul, the king of Israel, to deliver the fate of the entire nation into the hands of a youth who had never fought in battle before in his life. To me, the miracle was not so much that David killed Goliath, but rather that Saul let him try.

The Greek word translated *word* in Romans 10:17 is rhema, not logos. Faith comes from hearing the specific word (rhema) of the Lord to you regarding His will for the restoration of your marriage. In order to win the type of spiritual battles you will face, you need to know that you know that you know, as David did, that God's Word is specifically applicable to your marriage. You need a revelation of God's Word to you for your marriage. Sheer willpower and commitment will not be enough to hang in there long-term in spiritual warfare for your marriage. You must have the faith that comes out of having a revelation of God's will to heal your marriage. If you do not, you have a great potential to become legalistic and judgmental. If you attempt to take a stand for the healing and restoration of your marriage out of a sense of duty or obligation, rather than out of a love for God and your spouse, you will not bring life to yourself or others around you.

Apostle Paul tells us, "*Our adequacy is from God, Who also made us adequate as servants of a new covenant, not of the letter, but of the Spirit; for the letter kills, but the Spirit gives life,*" (II Corinthians 3:5b-6). I have met several people, having been separated from a spouse, who have taken a stand for the restoration of their marriage, but are so dogmatic, controlling, and issue oriented, that they are really obnoxious to be around.

Many in the body of Christ have entirely rejected the biblically correct idea of exercising faith for the restoration of a marriage when one spouse has left, because of contact with such people. When I have met such ones, I have often thought, "I can tell you why your spouse has left and doesn't want to return to the marriage. I have been around you for only fifteen minutes, and you have been so dogmatic and obnoxious that I don't care to be around you any more, either." Such people oftentimes have never really relinquished a spouse to God and are still trying to use God and biblical principles to force the spouse to return. This is counterproductive and brings forth death to this person and to all who come in contact with him/her.

The Lord showed me an analogy of the attitude of faith which we must have in order to effectively stand against the devil and with God for the resurrection of a marriage. A couple of centuries ago in Germany there was a group of powerfully missions-minded Christians, called the Moravians, raised up by God to carry the Gospel to the nations. There are still churches in many obscure parts of the world today which trace their founding heritage back to the Moravians. These people had an intense love for God and zeal to reach the world for Christ.

Some of the Moravians had such an intense zeal to carry the Gospel to unreached peoples who lived in lands where they were not allowed to go as missionaries that they sold themselves into slavery for the purpose of reaching people who were otherwise unreachable. These Christians, consumed with the zeal of Christ, gave up their money, their native language, their families and even their personal freedom for a lifetime in exchange for the opportunity to reach a few thousand people with the Gospel. To me, that is a pretty incredible sacrifice. When asked why they would do such a thing, they responded that they considered what they were giving up a very small price to pay in comparison with the eternal value of the people they would reach with the Gospel.

These people had a revelation from God of the reason why they were choosing to sell themselves into slavery. Suppose, however, that some other Christian heard about what the Moravians were doing and out of guilt, duty, and obligation felt like he should do the same. If he proceeded to do so, it would not be rooted in faith by the Spirit, but rather would simply be a work of the flesh, done in fulfillment of a religious obligation. The result of this, as we read in II Corinthians 3: 4-5, would be spiritual death. He would go around and tell others, "If you were a real Christian, you would sell yourself into slavery like I am doing." By so doing, he may even motivate others to do the same for the same wrong motive as he himself has. Such a man would probably not win many to the Lord as a slave. No one is attracted to be around someone who is doing something out of doctrine, obligation, or duty. Such a person continually emits spiritual death, not life.

My point is that it may be a great personal sacrifice to commit yourself unconditionally to God and your marriage covenant. This must, however, be done in faith, out of a love and zeal for God, His image, His name, and a trust in His great ability to transform people and resurrect marriages. Do not take a stand for your marriage against Satan simply out of duty or obligation. Continue to seek the face of God and let Him fill you with His love and zeal for His Kingdom as well as a supernatural love for your spouse, who may be, at this point, very difficult to love.

It is also important for you to know that you will meet many well meaning Christians, perhaps even in your own church, who do not have a revelation of the scriptures or the value of covenant in marriage. They will not understand why you do not simply abandon your marriage covenant and go find another partner. These people may be close friends of yours and with all sincerity of heart are trying to help you. If you continue to spend time around them and listen to them, they will discourage you and serve to weaken and nullify your faith in God's will and ability to do the impossible in your life and marriage.

Without realizing it, such people will become to you as the ten Hebrew spies of Numbers 13 were to Moses and the people of Israel. These ten spies, after spying out the land, reported that it would be wonderful to occupy, but that to conquer it would be impossible. Only Joshua and Caleb believed that God had told them to take the land and that He was well able to do "the impossible." The Bible records these ten spies as giving the sons of Israel "an evil report" (Num.13:32). What was evil about it? The report was true according to what they perceived with their natural senses. The evil part was the conclusion which they drew that was totally contrary to God's Word to them. He had not asked them to assess the feasibility of taking the land. He had already told them that He would dispossess these nations and drive them out ahead of Israel. These spies' conclusion not to go up and take the land because it was naturally and militarily impossible was an evil conclusion, because it was contrary, and, in direct disobedience, to the Word which God had given to Israel.

You will find many Christian people (even church leaders) who will tell you that you are crazy to remain faithful to your marriage covenant even after your spouse has departed. These people have accepted the worldly value of marriage as a contract and most probably do not hold many of the other values which we have talked about in earlier chapters. Please do not argue with them, as they will not understand what you are doing unless they accept the values which you accept. It is fruitless to debate scripture with someone who holds values entirely different from yours. Therefore, simply thank them for their concern and counsel, but do not continue to spend time around such people or listen further to their counsel. If you do, you will become discouraged as did the sons of Israel, fail to believe God for the impossible, and perish in the wilderness, never crossing the Jordan and taking the land. Instead, you must get around other people who hold the same values you do regarding marriage and spend time with them. You need to be around people who will encourage you not discourage you. Find other believers with the spirit of Joshua and Caleb, rather than those who have the attitude of the other ten spies.

STEP SIX

Get involved with others who can help and support you. There is a great temptation for many people who are experiencing crisis or difficulty to isolate and avoid contact with others. It will be very difficult for you to fight this battle alone. God never intended for us to have to fight this type of intense battle all by ourselves. Stay connected to your local church and talk with your pastor. One of the very best steps you can take is to locate and get involved with a **Covenant Keepers** group in your local area. Covenant Keepers is a ministry specifically designed to help and support people who are experiencing marital turmoil or separation. Because I believe that it is so important for you to be connected with other Christians who have experienced the type of crisis and battle that you are facing, I am including here in the body of the text the Covenant Keepers telephone number in Tulsa, OK, USA. (918) 743-0365. Please call this number right away so that you can locate a support group in your local area. Do not allow the devil to deceive you and keep you isolated.

STEP SEVEN

Attend a weekend FAMILY FOUNDATIONS BASIC SEMINAR. This is a seminar specifically designed to identify and remove root causes of marital conflict and family dysfunction. God intended for our marriages and families to be a great blessing to us. However, many times there are operating against us unseen emotional, spiritual, and even generational pressures which motivate us to mistreat and deeply wound those closest to us. As this occurs, our own marital or family relationships then become a source of intense pain and a curse to us rather than the blessing God intended. This seminar is designed to identify and bring healing to areas of past wounding in our lives which, when undealt with, continue to repeat themselves in our own lives and in the lives of our children. Many who have attended this seminar have experienced great release from emotional pain, change in habits and emotional response patterns, and radical transformation of marriage and family relationships from curse to blessing. Again, I feel that this is so important for you right at this time in your life, that I am including here in the text the ministry telephone number through which you may find information concerning the next seminar near you: In the USA (303) 797-1139.

QUESTIONS

I would now like to deal with some commonly asked questions regarding this biblical strategy of dealing with a spouse who does not want to remain in a marriage relationship. The strategy, again, is that you are taking a stand with God, against Satan, for the restoration of your broken marriage. You are committing yourself to remain single-minded and focused on Jesus, faithful to your marriage covenant in unilateral commitment to God and your spouse (regardless of the decisions of your spouse) until your marriage is reconciled or you or your spouse die. The attitude in so doing is not one of bearing a heavy burden, obligation, or duty. Instead, the attitude is one of faith toward God to do the impossible. The fruit of which is a joy and deep sense of fulfillment in serving Jesus Christ and His Kingdom. Great fulfillment comes through holding His image, name and the representation of His relationship with the Church in high esteem and honor among all who know you. Let us now turn our attention to several commonly asked questions.

1. My spouse has a free will. **Is it right for me to pray for the restoration of our marriage against his/her will?** In answer to this, it is critical to remember the scripture in Ephesians 6:10-12 that our battle is not against flesh and blood, but rather against deceptive forces of Satan and the kingdom of darkness. In the battle for your marriage, you are not fighting against your spouse, but rather against the forces of spiritual darkness who hate marriage and are seeking to destroy your family. Your spouse's will does not override God's will.

You need to view your spouse as a prisoner of war. He/she has been captured by the devil's deception and is not now in alignment with the will of God. Therefore, there is a need to intercede for the deceptive, demonic strongholds in his/her thinking to be pulled down and the thoughts to come into alignment with the will of Jesus Christ (II Corinthians 10:3-5).

This is no different than when we intercede for a young pregnant woman who is planning to murder her baby through abortion. Is it right to pray and exercise faith against her will for her to carry her baby full term to birth? Of course it is. If she has been deceived by Satan to believe that aborting her baby is an option, then she is a prisoner of war and needs some spiritual warriors to conduct battle on her behalf against the forces of darkness to tear down the demonic strongholds in her mind which are in opposition to the will of God.

You must realize that although you cannot force your spouse to make a right choice, you certainly can pray and exercise your faith for the will of God to be done in your marriage and your spouse's life. This is an extremely powerful influence which significantly impacts the ability of the forces of darkness to continue to deceive your spouse.

2. **How long should I continue to remain faithful to my marriage covenant and believe God for the restoration of my**

marriage? The answer to this, of course, is very simple if you have already accepted the value of covenant in marriage. You are committed to your spouse and marriage covenant until you are parted by death. There is no time limit on the work of God. It is similar to believing God for physical healing. A person with cancer may ask, "How long do I have to believe God for my healing?" The answer is very simple: just until you are healed. You may stop exercising faith for healing when one of two things happen, either you are healed or you die. There are no other options. If you give in to the sickness and accept it, then you are submitting to the devil (the author of sickness) against God. This same is true regarding the healing of your marriage.

3. **What if my spouse divorces me and remarries someone else?** Many people are able to stand in faith for the healing of their marriage up until the actual divorce is finalized. No doubt, this is a very discouraging experience, but is by no means the end, unless you are a reactive, not a proactive person. If you have committed yourself to emotional maturity, to be a proactive person, then your choices are not predicated upon the choices of your spouse. His/her choice of divorce does not affect your unilateral commitment to God and your marriage covenant one bit. Your choice is independent of the choices of your spouse.

Suppose your spouse should go ahead and remarry another person. Most people, even Christians, would tell you that it is over, and you should forget your spouse, go on with your life and find someone else to marry. Very few people understand a unilateral covenant commitment, and even fewer people actually live their life proactively, not predicating their choices upon reaction to the choices of others. However, if you truly acknowledge the unilateral covenant commitment you made before God and to your spouse in your wedding vows, and if you are truly a person of integrity, your spouse's choice to remarry does not affect your covenant commitment at all.

The divorce decree issued by man in no way nullifies the covenant of marriage before God. There are still at least two witnesses attesting to the covenant made on your wedding day, you and God. The fact that your marriage partner refuses to acknowledge the covenant does not change the fact that your marriage is still a covenant before God until death do you part. Any other "marriage" your spouse may enter into is a non-covenant "marriage" which, as we have seen, Jesus categorizes as adultery. Your job is to continue to pray against the deception of your spouse, for the termination of the non-covenant adulterous relationship, and for the resurrection of your covenant marriage.

Some say, "You mean you are encouraging people to pray now for the breakup and divorce of another marriage." Not at all. I am encouraging people to pray for the termination of an adulterous relationship and for the restoration of a broken marriage. Those who would say such a thing (you may expect to encounter many of them who will seek to discourage you) usually have tacitly embraced the Erasmian position on marital relationship, do not understand covenant, and thus do not see the second marriage as sin against God. The fact of the matter is that this non-covenant "marriage" is not a legitimate marriage any more than a homosexual or incestual "marriage" would be. I would take the same position regarding either a homosexual, incestual, or adulterous "marriage." These are not legitimate marriages before God. Consequently, as believers in Christ, we should intercede for persons engaged in such illegitimate relationships, for them to be delivered from their deception, convicted of their sin, and to terminate their wrong relationships. This is consistent with the dealings of God in the days of Ezra when He commanded the men of Israel to divorce their non-covenant wives. From your standpoint, if your spouse remarries, this changes nothing regarding your position or choices. You should continue to pray for conviction of sin and your spouse to come to repentance.

Many times couples who have been divorced and remarried to other people have asked me, "What does it really mean to repent of the sin of adultery in remarriage?" I have responded in the following way. Firstly, I believe there are two areas of sin to be dealt with. 1) Divorce and 2) Remarriage. Covenant breaking is the primary issue of which there must be repentance. Covenant breaking occurs with divorce for the initiating partner. It occurs for a "victim" or recipient of divorce at the time of his/her own remarriage. Jesus calls this adultery. This sin of adultery through remarriage then is not unforgivable, but rather must be dealt with just as is any other sin, through repentance and forgiveness.

Repentance means to change your attitude, stop justifying yourself and come into agreement with Jesus Christ. It means to turn around and go the other direction. However, repentance is not the only issue at hand. Restitution must also be made. If I steal another man's car, it is not enough that I merely repent, agree with God by saying I was wrong to do so and continue to possess and drive the man's car. Restitution requires me at least to return the man's car to him and to pay him for all damage and inconvenience he has incurred as a result of my actions. Biblical restitution often required not only restoration of property but a manifold repayment (4 or 7 times). I believe that how one makes restitution for the sin of adultery through remarriage depends on whether or not there exists a former spouse who was not in agreement with the divorce and has been believing God for the restoration of his/her marriage.

When there is a former spouse who has remained faithful in covenant and is desirous of restoration of the original marriage, then true **repentance** requires one to turn from justification of the remarriage as a legitimate or right thing to do, to agreement with Jesus that the act of remarriage was sin against the Lord and the former spouse, and constitutes adultery. **Restitution**, in this case, requires one to terminate the adulterous "marriage" and return to the original covenant partner.

We see a few examples of such in the Bible. One such example is the restoration of Michal, David's wife back to him. Saul had wrongly taken Michal from David and given her to another man. After the death of Saul, Michal was once again restored to David, her rightful husband, (II Samuel 3:14-15). Another such example is the restoration of Gomer to her covenant husband, Hosea, out of a non-covenant, adulterous marriage (Hosea 2-3).

Many have used the passage in Deuteronomy 24:1-4 to claim that once an errant spouse is remarried in a subsequent adulterous "marriage" but later repents and terminates this adulterous relationship that he/she is not to return in marriage to the covenant spouse. However, upon simply reading the passage, it is very clear that this passage has nothing to do with the above mentioned situation.

> *"When a man takes a wife and marries her, and it happens that she finds no favor in his eyes because he has found some indecency in her, and he writes her a certificate of divorce and puts it in her hand and sends her out from his house, and she leaves his house and goes and becomes another man's wife, and if the latter husband turns against her and writes her a certificate of divorce and puts it in her hand and sends her out of his house, or if the latter husband dies who took her to be his wife, then her former husband who sent her away is not allowed to take her again to be his wife, since she has been defiled; for that is an abomination before the Lord, and you shall not bring sin on the land which the Lord your God gives you as an inheritance* (Deuteronomy 24:1-4).

This passage is not talking about a faithful, covenant-keeping partner's not being allowed to receive back in marriage an unfaithful, straying partner. It is, rather, clearly dealing with the case in which a man has divorced his wife due to some sort of sexual impurity on her part, and she has remarried another. In this case, if she should subsequently become single again for any reason, the former husband is not allowed to take her a second time as his wife. In other words, if a man divorces his wife due to her sexual impurity and she remarries, he does not later have a right to change his mind and receive her back as his wife again. Thus, this passage has nothing whatsoever to do with a faithful covenant keeper believing God for the restoration of his/her marriage. It may have to do with a covenant breaking husband's initiating divorce and a covenant breaking wife's remarrying.

However, as I have studied this passage, I don't think that it pertains even to events occurring during the course of a marriage after the wedding night at all. Rather, I believe that Moses is speaking here about a man's right to annul a marriage if he finds **on his wedding night** that he has been defrauded, and his wife is not a virgin.

Alfred Edersheim in his insightful book on Jewish historical culture writes:

"Marriage with a maiden was commonly celebrated on a Wednesday afternoon, which allowed the first days of the week for preparation, and enabled the husband, if he had a charge to prefer against the previous chastity of his bride, to make immediate complaint before the local Sanhedrim, which sat every Thursday. On the other hand, the marriage of a widow was celebrated on Thursday afternoon, which left three days of the week for 'rejoicing with her.'"[1]

The language used in Deuteronomy 24 is: *"because he hath found some uncleanness in her."* I believe that most likely, this phrase is referring to the case in which a woman was found not to be a virgin on her wedding night, rather than the case in which she has committed adultery at some later date in the course of the marriage. This is evident in view of the regular enforcement of the death penalty at that time for the commission of adultery. There would have been no need for Moses to discuss the option of writing a certificate of divorce in the case of adultery. The adulterer would have been dead and thus unavailable to be divorced. Therefore, it seems highly unlikely that this Deuteronomy 24 passage would have anything to do with events occurring subsequent to the initial wedding night. In any case, it is absolutely clear that this passage has nothing whatsoever to do with an errant remarried, covenant breaking spouse then repenting, making restitution and returning to a faithful covenant keeping spouse.

Thus, when there is a former spouse who has remained faithful to his/her original marriage vows, even in the face of divorce and remarriage of a partner, it is indeed right for that person to pray for his/her mate to be delivered from deception, terminate the adulterous "marriage" and return to the original covenant marriage. I believe, however, that the principle expressed in the Deuteronomy 24 passage would preclude a former spouse, who has not all along kept his/her marital vows, believing God for the restoration of the original marriage, from subsequently exercising the right to change his/her mind and months or years later invade a subsequent marriage, demanding that it be terminated and the former spouse return to the original marriage in the name of "restitution." I believe that restitution in this situation should be handled entirely differently. For an expanded treatment of this subject, see my book *Marriage: Covenant or Contract.*[2]

4. **What if my spouse is seriously abusive?** Am I expected to just remain in an abusive situation and do nothing? First of all, as we begin to address this topic, it is important to define what we mean by abuse. This word has become very popular these days and is applied to everything from attempted murder to being spoken to

in a cross voice. The literal meaning of the word abuse is simply to be misused or used for something other than the created purpose. With this definition in mind, every time a husband and wife act selfishly or speak harshly toward one another there is "abuse" taking place.

Scripture gives us some insight into how we are to respond to mistreatment in I Peter 2:18-24.

> *"Servants, be submissive to your masters with all respect, not only to those who are good and gentle, but also to those who are unreasonable, for this finds favor, if for the sake of conscience toward God a man bears up under sorrows when suffering unjustly. For what credit is there if, when you sin and are harshly treated, you endure it with patience? But if when you do what is right and suffer for it you patiently endure it, this finds favor with God. For you have been called for this purpose, since Christ also suffered for you leaving you an example for you to follow in His steps, Who committed no sin, nor was any deceit found in His mouth; and while being reviled, He did not revile in return; while suffering He uttered no threats, but kept entrusting Himself to Him Who judges righteously; and He himself bore our sins in His body on the cross, that we might die to sin and live to righteousness; for by His wounds you were healed*" (I Peter 2:18-24).

This passage outlines the attitude which we are to take when mistreated. The Greek word used in verse 18 and translated "unreasonable" is the word *skolios*. You have probably heard of an English derivative of this word, scoliosis of the spine. Scolios means crooked, bent, perverted, twisted, etc. Peter here tells us that a servant is not only to submit to a master who is good and gentle, but also to one who is crooked, bent, perverted, and twisted. He says that doing so finds favor, which is actually the Greek word *charis*, which means grace, with God. Thus, God's grace and favor are poured out upon one who suffers unjustly.

Peter then goes on to point out that Jesus, Himself, suffered injustice and left us an example to walk in. Jesus did not rise up against injustice nor did He run from it. He conquered it through death to self and resurrection. The last part of verse 24 is frequently quoted and applied to anything and everything: "*...for by His stripes you were healed.*" This verse is frequently applied to physical healing, the validity of which I do not dispute, but taken in context, this verse is actually talking about something entirely different. This verse is referring to healing from the physical, emotional, and any other damage which has come to you as a result of submitting yourself to a *scolios* (unreasonable) leader. Thus when you are harmed in relationship, Jesus' blood was shed for you and by His stripes you were healed. I believe that this would certainly apply to a spouse.

Let me then summarize what Peter tells us in this passage. Firstly, he tells us to get out of idolatry and empower God, not man, as the determiner of your identity and destiny. When you have done so, then you can be empowered by the supernatural love and grace of God to remain in relationship with and even submit to someone who is unreasonable and even twisted or perverse. When you then suffer unjustly, trusting God and not man, you find favor with God, learn to die to sin and live to righteousness, and you can expect to receive healing by Jesus' wounds at the cross for any damage you incur in the process.

This is the attitude with which we are to approach an unreasonable, abusive husband or wife. You may ask, "How far do I go in doing so?" I would answer this in two ways. The first is that you must not violate your own conscience or do that which is morally wrong in submission to or agreement with your spouse. If you are being asked or forced, for example, to participate in sexual perversion, murder, stealing, pornography, or molesting a child, you should firmly decline.

If this type of illegal activity is being practiced by your spouse, you should immediately report such to your pastor or other spiritual authorities, as well as to the police or civil authorities. A process will then be started by which you and your spouse can get help. You should not try to deal with this in isolation by yourself. You need immediate intervention and help from others. The lie of the devil is that the authorities will deal too strongly with your spouse, and so you should not expose him/her to the authorities because of your love. NO! Just the opposite is true. If you love him/her, you will care enough to bring sin into the light so that he/she can receive some effectual, long-term help. The first step is to expose the reality of the situation to your pastor, pray about it with him, and let him help you get a plan from God to contact any other necessary authorities.

Secondly, if you are being physically threatened, battered, or raped, again, do not hide this reality. Go immediately to your pastor and then to the civil authorities and expose the situation. You will probably need some ongoing ministry, yourself, for a time. I would encourage you then to remain in or separate from that physical situation according to your faith. Most people will need to physically separate from the spouse. However, if you have faith and clear rhema revelation from God for your physical protection and to remain living physically with such a spouse, then continue according to your faith. If you do not, do not feel guilty. Just separate for a time until your spouse can receive help and be healed.

If a husband, for example, is found to be sexually molesting a daughter, that situation should be immediately reported to church and civil authorities. That husband must be immediately removed physically from that home and may not return until he has received significant ministry, and there is certainty that he is free of such behavior, and it will never happen again.

In such severe cases in which there is a need for physical separation between husband and wife, this is not for the purpose of abandoning relationship and looking for someone else. It is even more critical at this point to pray and exercise faith for the deliverance and healing of an abusive spouse. Your spouse may be like the Gadarene demoniac of Mark 5 out of whom Jesus cast a legion of demons and totally set the man free. Jesus can do the same for your spouse. Many times it is the faith and effectual prayer of a faithful spouse that releases God's power to accomplish such.

I believe that the life of David perhaps exemplifies very well a proper attitude and response to injustice and abuse.

> *"And Saul tried to pin David to the wall with a spear, but he slipped away out of Saul's presence, so that he stuck the spear into the wall. And David fled and escaped that night"* (I Samuel 19:10).

For the next decade Saul hunted David and tried to kill him. This sounds to me like pretty serious abuse. David however, never abandoned his love for Saul or his relationship with him. David continued to honor Saul as his king and the Lord's anointed. Even when he had two opportunities to kill Saul and rid his life of the torment and terror of being continually hunted, out of his love and respect for Saul and his honor for God, he would not harm him. If, at any point, Saul would have been delivered of his hatred and jealousy of David and been willing to reconcile their relationship, David's heart was ready and continually open to Saul. Even though David could not remain in the palace and allow Saul to pin him to the wall with a spear, he never divorced Saul in relationship, denounced him as king, or attempted to harm him in any way.

Unfortunately, in the relationship between David and Saul, Saul never was set free, and he went to his grave having never reconciled his relationship with David. Although this relationship between David and Saul was not one of husband and wife, I believe that David's attitude toward Saul is a good picture of the correct attitude that one must have toward a severely abusive spouse. No matter what a spouse has done, covenant faithfulness on the part of the non-offending spouse is a powerful tool which the Lord can utilize toward the healing of the offending spouse and ultimately the marriage.

5. **What if my spouse is a practicing homosexual?** The answer to this is very similar to what we have just covered above regarding abuse. This is not an excuse to abandon the marriage. However, if your spouse is involved in any extramarital sexual relationships, homosexual or heterosexual, you run the risk of contracting sexually transmitted diseases, including AIDS. You may rightly choose to abstain from sexual relationship with your spouse until such time as he/she is delivered from the promiscuity. During this time, continue to pray for your spouse, believing God for total freedom from bondage and retain the love and open-hearted attitude that David had toward Saul.

---

[1]Edersheim, Alfred, *op. cit.* p.151
[2]Hill, Craig, *Marriage: Covenant or Contract*, Northglenn, Co., Harvest Books and Publishing, 1993

Chapter 5

God's Faithfulness to a Covenant Keeper

On March 7th, 1982, after twenty-two years of marriage, Tom Bearry, out of the clear blue sky, called his wife Lou by telephone and announced that he wanted a divorce. Lou was shocked and emotionally devastated. She knew that they had some problems in their marriage, but she had no idea that Tom wanted to divorce her. Following is an amazing miracle story of the power of God, the faithfulness of a covenant keeping spouse, and the resurrection of a dead marriage.

TOM: Although Lou was shocked and devastated when I called her and told her that I wanted a divorce, this was not at all a spur of the moment decision for me, but rather was something that I had been contemplating and actually planning for a long time. I want to share with you some of my background which may help you to understand some of what God has to do in you and your spouse in order to restore your marriage. Divorce was not something new or unfamiliar to me. You see, I grew up in a home in which my parents were divorced. I came from a background of childhood abuse, incest, and abandonment. My parents were not committed to Jesus Christ and thus did not impart many godly, moral values to me, so I had a very distorted view of right and wrong. I became my own authority to determine my own sense of morality.

When I was 18 years old, I was given twenty-four hours to get out of the house. Having nowhere else to go and no other plans, I joined the military. I figured that I had a strong-willed, independent personality and had been working since age nine, so I could certainly make it on my own in the military. Since I had never been made to feel that I was of any worth in my family, I was out to prove myself to be a real man through achievement in the military. My life revolved around my accomplishments.

Three and a half years later when Lou and I met, I was a 190 pound, crew-cut, career military black belt in Karate, who could put my hands through six inches of wood, and I let everyone know that you had better not mess with me! I did not realize at that time, that in reality, my life was nothing but an empty shell, and that the tough, confident exterior image was only a cover-up for the deep inner emptiness and insecurity. I thought that I had my act together, but emotionally I was severely crippled. When we married, neither Lou nor I had any understanding of the emotional baggage which we both brought into the marriage. I had an intense focus on career achievement and a deep need to be needed. Lou saw me as her hero and deeply needed me. So we married, looking to each other to meet needs which we later found out that only God could meet.

Since I had my sights set on being an officer, after Lou and I were married, I temporarily left the military to go to college. While in college, Lou and I had three children. It was a difficult time as I was working to put myself through college, studying and trying to be a husband and father. Lou grew to be totally reliant upon me emotionally. Even though it was very stressful, I "knew" I could do anything I set my will to. I said, "I can do it," and I believed it. So did Lou. However, I did not realize that my need to be the tough, strong, decisive knight in shining armor to Lou had fueled her insecurity and allowed her to make me her god rather than her husband. She became totally dependent upon me for everything.

Shortly after graduating from college, I went back into the military and received my commission. By this time, Lou's emotional dependence upon me was becoming very draining to me. No one can live up to god-hood, and I had found that Lou was depending upon me for 100% of her existence. All decisions regarding anything we did were entirely mine. As my emotional energy became more and more depleted through my marriage relationship with Lou, I lost the feeling of romantic love for her. I still cared for Lou, but I began to look at her more as a sister than a wife. The marriage for me was becoming an endurance contest, and I found myself seeking ways to escape from the emotional drain. I began entertaining thoughts of leaving my marriage.

It was not long until I was no longer just entertaining thoughts, but was laying concrete plans. Even though I was not a Christian, I was a generous sort of person, and I thought of myself as living a better life than most Christians I knew. Therefore, there were several things by way of preparation that had to come to pass before I could leave Lou. Even though I didn't love Lou as my wife, but more as a sister, I wanted to be able to take care of my "sister" financially when I left. I had to be earning enough to support two families. By this time, we had four children, and I wanted to stick around long enough for my boys to have their feet on the ground and their heads on straight. I wanted to make sure that they were stable enough to make it through the emotional trauma of their parents' divorce. I have since learned that one is never old enough or stable enough to make it through a divorce of parents. God never intended for any child to have to experience such a traumatic ripping and tearing.

As I mentioned earlier, Lou was very weak emotionally and totally dependent upon me. Since I wanted her to be able to make it as well, I kept encouraging her to go to church and Bible studies. I wanted her to get into relationship with God and get on her own two feet so that I could leave and get on with my life. My marriage had become nothing but a giant millstone around my neck.

Finally, in 1978, after we had been married for 18 years, it seemed like all these things had come together. I now had a salary which would allow me to support two families. My kids were now mature enough to understand and survive the trauma, and Lou had found the Lord. There was only one last thing which I wanted to accomplish before I left. I wanted to relocate my family to Austin, Texas, which was only ninety miles from where Lou was born, where I knew that she and the kids would have plenty of family support from her relatives. The Air Force had a provision at that time that if you volunteered to spend twelve months in a remote location, such as above the Arctic Circle, that the Air Force would then relocate you to the the base of your choice. Consequently, I took such an assignment and then relocated my family to Bergstrom Air Force Base in Austin, Texas. I built Lou a nice home and prepared to leave. Two years later an opportunity for assignment in Europe came up, so I volunteered.

In preparation for my assignment in Europe, I had to attend a special staff training course in Mississippi. I had planned to go to Europe, leave Lou in Austin and never return to the marriage. However, I had not yet had the courage to tell Lou and at this point, she still thought that she was going with me. Within just a few days after arriving in Mississippi, Satan brought into my life the catalyst which stimulated my phone call to Lou. I had not been looking for another woman, but suddenly there she was, and she was everything that I thought that I had ever wanted in a woman. Shortly after meeting her in 1982, I phoned Lou and told her that she would not be going to Europe with me and that I wanted a divorce.

LOU: When I got the phone call, I couldn't believe what I was hearing. I knew that there were marital problems and that Tom was not happy, but I had no idea that it was to the point of divorce. I had often queried, "Tom, something's wrong." But he would respond, "No, everything's fine. I love you." Just a little over a week before on February 27th, our anniversary, Tom had sent me flowers from Mississippi. Several days later, I had remarked, "I hope Tom's love for me never dies like these flowers are dying." Three days later he called for a divorce. I was totally shattered.

I cried out, "God, what am I going to do?" I had four teenage sons to raise and emotionally I was still a child myself. I had been totally dependent upon Tom, and now he was suddenly gone. I had indeed met the Lord prior to this, but I was a brand new baby Christian without any Bible teaching or ability to feed myself on the Word of God. However, God began working in my life right away, even beyond my knowledge. The first thing He did was to delay the divorce process. Normally it takes six weeks for a divorce to become final in Texas. When we appeared to sign the papers, the lawyer told Tom that because of my emotional state we would have to wait to sign the papers in order for my signature to be valid.

At that time I didn't know where to go or what to do. I went to the Catholic church for prayer meeting and any time the doors were opened. It was there that I found a measure of comfort and relief from the intense emotional pain. At that time, I was not aware of any support groups, books, or ministries for people facing the trauma I was facing, but the Holy Spirit was my teacher. The only prayer I knew was, "Holy Spirit, please carry me; I can't walk." Tom, of course, thought that I would hate him and never want to see him again, but the Holy Spirit immediately gave me an unconditional, agape love for him. Since I had lived my married life as an emotional cripple, totally dependent upon Tom, God was now taking me through the process of learning to trust Him instead of Tom. This proved to be a very lengthy and painful emotional process whereby I had to start out learning to crawl before I could even walk.

Meanwhile, God had His hand upon my sons. They were devastated just as I was. They not only lost their dad, but they lost their mom for quite some time as well. I was emotionally incapacitated and had no ability to be there for my sons. They saw their mom totally broken, crying much of the time, so they didn't want to add to my pain by bringing their problems home.

TOM: After my training in Mississippi I returned to Austin for about six weeks before I left for Europe. During that period of time, Lou asked me to go with her for marriage counseling, to which I agreed. I thought that then I could say that I had tried, I had received counseling, but that it didn't work. In the course of this counseling, I had an ordained minister tell me that he admired me. It took courage, he said, to do what I was doing, and that it was time for me to get on with my life and file for divorce. "At this point, we switch from marriage counseling to divorce counseling," he said. He was then going to counsel us on how to conduct a successful divorce.

Another counselor told me, "It takes guts to do what you're doing, Tom. I admire you for it and I think it's time for you to go ahead and file for divorce. Your marriage is obviously irreconcilable." I believe that if I had received good counseling, from the Word of God, there is a chance that I might have reconsidered and stayed. However, all I received, even from ministers in the church, was worldly counsel based on circumstances and emotion. No one gave me the Word of God, or hope that Jesus Christ could change anything. I learned that you must be careful whom you receive counsel from.

After six weeks, I left for Europe without Lou or my family. Because Lou had been too emotionally unstable to sign the divorce papers while I was in Austin, we were not at that time legally divorced. I did not actively pursue the divorce because I basically had what I wanted. The pressure was off. I had told Lou, and I was now out of the marriage. The other woman with whom I had become romantically involved quit her job in Mississippi and followed me to Europe.

Over the next couple years I would phone Lou periodically from Europe just to check up on my boys. She would frequently tell me that she still loved me and that one day I was coming home to my family. I simply told her she was crazy, that she should get on with her life and to forget about me. I had hoped that she would get over the pain and go find someone else, remarry, and leave me alone. She did not. Instead, she continued to insist that one day our marriage would be restored.

In 1984 I had an experience with the Lord in which I was born again. However, I did not grow strong in the Lord, but instead returned right back into the pigpen. I justified what I was doing and bought into Satan's lie that God would not want me to be unhappy and return to a miserable situation in my marriage with Lou. Having returned from Europe in 1984, I was still involved in a romantic relationship with the woman I had met in Mississippi. I finally decided to go ahead and marry her in the autumn of 1985. This then became the catalyst for me to legally finalize the divorce with Lou. When I sent Lou the papers, she did not even contest the divorce, but simply told me, "It doesn't matter anyway, you're coming home." I don't think she even read the papers I sent her. She just signed them and sent them back. I was going to get the divorce whether she wanted it or not, so we were legally divorced in October of 1985, and within two weeks I was married to the other woman.

LOU: After even the Christian counselor told Tom to go ahead and file for divorce and he then left for Europe without me, it appeared that my marriage was certainly over. At that point in time I did not know what the Bible said about marriage as a covenant, or any other teaching. We were merely trying to survive emotionally and as a family. In the two years before Tom had left I continually read Psalm 34 from the Living Bible. I didn't know at that time that God had given me that Psalm, which I continued to read after Tom left, to prepare me and strengthen me during the time of emotional trauma.

Nine months after Tom left for Europe, one day while I was in the school library, I heard the Lord audibly speak to me. "He's coming home, Lou," He said. I heard the Lord speak this out loud three times. This is the only time anything like this has ever happened to me. I had never before, or since, heard the Lord speak in an audible voice. This greatly encouraged my faith, however, and I later learned that faith is what activates the power of God on the earth. I really did not know the God who had spoken to me, but from that time, I diligently began to seek after Him. It was at this point that the growing conviction began to come that no matter what the circumstance appeared to be, God Almighty was working in Tom's heart and that one day he would come home.

Even in spite of hearing God's voice audibly, I still wanted to quit a million times because it is hard to stand in faith. I had days when I just wanted to die, and other days when I was consumed with anger and bitterness toward Tom. But underneath it all was the underlying agape love of God for me and the supernatural agape love which God had given me for Tom. You have to have that love from God for you and in your heart for your spouse in order to continue to stand against Satan for the healing of your marriage. It is often very difficult to die to your flesh when you are having all sorts of problems and your mate seems to be prospering and having a good time. You walk through the bitterness and the hatred until God comes and heals you and makes you a brand new person. That's what He did for me. Over a period of time, He took my broken heart and put it back together piece by piece.

Over that first year God brought people into my life who began to help me grow spiritually. I began to go to a church where there was strong Bible teaching. In the second year after Tom left, God led me to a church with a strong emphasis on faith in God's Word and the supernatural power of the Holy Spirit. By this time, I knew what the Bible said about covenant, God's supernatural ability to change people and heal marriages. I thought I would receive strong support from my church in uniting their faith with mine for the resurrection of my marriage. I was wrong. Instead, the greatest discouragement and lack of understanding I received was from the church. Church leaders as well as Christian friends continually told me that I was living in denial of reality and that I needed to forget Tom and get on with my life. Find some other godly man and marry him, I was told. When I would tell them about hearing the Lord say that Tom was coming home, instead of encouraging me, they would ask, "What if he never comes home?"

At one time, I had taken off my wedding ring for about a month, but the Lord told me to put it back on. People would say, "Are you married?" I would say, "Yes, my husband is on a long TDY" (which in the military means temporary duty). Those were acts of faith that helped me to continue to say, "I'm married."

God gave me the grace and strength to continue to be a covenant keeper even with very little support from other Christians. When Tom remarried in 1985, the senior pastor of my church even told me to forget Tom and go on with my life. There was no hope. But I couldn't quit believing God. By this time, I knew that I knew that I knew what the Bible said and what God had personally spoken to me. It's hard to have church leaders and your own pastor tell you that you're crazy and missing God, but I had heard it from the big Boss. God had spoken to me and nobody could say otherwise.

Obviously when Tom remarried it was an emotional blow to me. I was deeply hurt. On the day he remarried, a church leader had deeply discouraged me again. She had said, "Well, you don't still want him to come home now, do you?" When I got home, I cried out to the Lord, "God I know that you still want me to remain faithful to Tom, but I need to hear it from someone else." God answered my prayer in about twenty minutes. My second son, who had had a birthday that day, came in and said, "Mom, look how far we've come and how much we've grown. We've done this and that. Mom, you're not a quitter." That was all I needed to continue on, at that point.

Even though Tom had remarried I was so certain by this time what the will of the Lord was for our marriage that I was not devastated. I knew that God had been a witness to the covenant of marriage that Tom and I had made, and that the relationship that Tom had with this other woman was adulterous. Because God and I were still faithful witnesses to the original covenant of Holy Matrimony between Tom and me, Tom was not free to enter into a second covenant. God could not witness his adulterous "marriage." Because I had not broken or released our marriage covenant, in God's sight Tom was still married to me. I continued to pray and stand against the deception of the enemy in Tom's life and to believe in the power of God to resurrect our marriage. The fact that Tom had remarried had not changed, but only delayed, what I knew to be the will of God for our marriage. I knew that Tom had to come completely to the end of himself before he could return home. I believed that this adulterous marriage would ultimately help accomplish that purpose.

When I first began my walk with God as a covenant keeper in Tom's absence, my primary concern was for my own emotional well being. I was just trying to survive. The focus was on Tom's returning for my benefit. The more I grew in the Lord, the more I could see that the purpose in my remaining faithful to my marriage vows was not for my benefit, but rather that Jesus might be glorified through my life and faithfulness. When you first start out, the marriage is sort of on the top of the scale and God is on the bottom, but as you grow and receive more and more healing and love, the scale flips. Many times people start out wanting to use God to restore a marriage, but as they grow, they come to recognize that instead, the goal is to allow God to use their faithfulness to glorify His name and expand His kingdom on the earth. The restored marriage can then become a testimony to glorify God rather than simply the means to meet the needs of an insecure and selfish spouse.

Over the next couple of years, my walk with the Lord was growing stronger and stronger. I had the inner peace that I could remain single forever, and if Tom never came home, I was living for God's glory. (Why would I want him home? I had a very peaceful life.) I no longer needed Tom in order to be a whole person. God had done a miraculous work in my heart and brought me into a peace and security in Him. In November of 1987 I had gone to a Christian retreat and had a very strong sense that Tom was coming home in 1988. I thought that it would be really nice if we could get married again on our original wedding date, February 27th; and we did. Again, nobody believed me when I said that I believed that our marriage would come back together in 1988. As we were getting dressed for our wedding, our oldest son said, "Mom, I'm sorry we didn't believe you." I said, "That's alright. Your dad didn't either."

TOM: When Lou said that I hadn't believed that our marriage would ever be restored she was right. I didn't believe it even up until the very end when the deception was lifted and the truth became clear. Over the years we had maintained telephone contact because I wanted to know what was transpiring in the lives of my boys. Every now and then, she would tell me that she was not looking for a new spouse and that she was standing with God in covenant against Satan's destruction of our marriage and waiting for me to be delivered from deception and return home. I told her that she was crazy and should get on with her life. She would say, "No, I'm standing and you're coming home." Even after I got married, she said, "You're coming home." "Not this century!" I replied. I told her to go out and meet and marry a good, Spirit-filled Christian man. She did. Me!

I had retired from the military in April of 1986 and went into business for myself. By the end of 1987 my business and my second marriage had begun crumbling around me. I discovered that when you don't have your personal life lined up with God's ways, nothing else works. I only lived about two miles from my office, but I had gotten to the point to where I regularly consumed a six-pack of beer between the office and home just to get up the courage to walk in the door in the evening.

Finally, on January 7th, 1988, late at night, I got down on my knees, completely drunk and began crying out to God. My marriage and my business were in shambles, and I said, "God, I blew it. I give my life to you. I cannot handle it." A calm came over me as I went to bed that night. The next morning, I awoke with a sense of purpose and direction. I moved out of the home I shared with my non-covenant wife, moved into an apartment, and immediatedly filed for divorce.

The following Saturday I was sitting in my office around noon, reading the paper when all of the sudden I got this overwhelming urge that I had to get to Austin. I knew that one of my sons was in trouble and I had to get there. At this time I hadn't seen Lou for about two and a half years, and I thought that I wouldn't mind seeing her again. There was also a particular pastor in Austin whom I had not heard in some time, and I thought that I might like to hear him preach at church the next day, so by one o'clock I was in the car on my way to Austin.

Fourteen and a half hours later at 3:30 a.m., I arrived in Austin. Lou had no idea that I was coming and the purpose of my trip was not really to see her, but just to see what was going on with my sons. At 3:30 a.m. I called, woke her up and asked, "Do you want to go to church with me in the morning?" She screamed and asked where I was. I replied that I was about five minutes down the road. I found later that God had really set me up on this one. She didn't know that I was coming home then, and I had no intention of coming home to stay. I was just coming for the day to see how my sons were and then returning right back to my apartment. God however, was working in the spiritual realm and He had other plans for me. Before I left that weekend, we had already decided that we were going to reconcile and be remarried.

When I returned home that Sunday morning, it became very evident to me that God had done a major work of transformation in my wife. She was not at all the same woman whom I had left some six years earlier. There were several small things that impressed me. Before I had left, one of the major issues about which I used to get quite irritated was the cleanliness of the house. When I returned that Sunday morning, even though there had recently been a large party in the house, it was clean and very much in order.

I was shocked to find that Lou really had kept her marriage vows to me. She had been entirely faithful to me even in very little things. She was my wife, and for the entire six years had conducted herself as my wife. There had been no strange men in the house. When I had called in the middle of the night, there was no mad scramble to quickly get someone out of the house. When I arrived, my coffee mugs were still on the kitchen shelves. My photograph was still over the mantle. My clothes were still hanging in the closet, just where I had left them six years ago. Even the bills had been kept in my name all that time. My telephone account still shows uninterrupted service in my name since 1978. The point is, I felt at home. I'm not saying that that is going to bring your mate home, but when your mate does come home, you don't want any unnecessary obstacles or barriers there. I was able to kick off my shoes, sit back in my Lazy Boy chair and say to myself, "Feels good!"

My wife had left the door totally open for me. When I came home, it felt like I belonged. So when your spouse comes home, his or her front door key has to still fit the lock. Their clothes, and possessions should not be in a box in the attic somewhere. If it hurts too much to have the photograph up and possessions prominently displayed, I can understand putting them down until the hurt has lessened. However, if you have children, whether it hurts or not, they have to know that they still have a father and mother intact, even if one of them is temporarily indisposed as a prisoner of war.

After I arrived at the house early that Sunday morning, we stayed up and talked the rest of the night. After church we talked again all Sunday afternoon. By the time Sunday evening came, I asked Lou if she could forgive me and if she would receive me back. There was no hesitation on her part. We then talked to the boys and found that they agreed unanimously for the reconciliation. So by the time I left at the end of the weekend, it was only to close down my business, and gather my possessions to return to Austin. We were then remarried to each other on our anniversary, February 27th, 1988.

One of the motivations which the Lord used to draw me home was a concern for one of our sons. My concern did indeed turn out to be valid. When I arrived home, even though no one knew it, my son was deeply involved in the drug world and was dying. He liked street drugs, had tested them all, and as a result of their influence had given up on life. There was drug paraphernalia all over the house, but neither Lou nor I recognized it. Three months after I came home, I was talking with my son one day about career and school when he exclaimed, "Dad, you don't understand. I'm not going to be alive in three years." About three days later, he went off the deep end into a total breakdown, and spent 103 days locked up in the Austin State Hospital. The doctors said that he would never live a normal life again. By that time Lou's faith had rubbed off on me and we told the world and the doctors, "No, God has another plan for our son." Our son today is off drugs and in college, with almost a 4.0 grade point average.

I want to tell you that your stand with God against the destruction of the devil, for the restoration of your marriage may be far more important than you think. Your choices may have far-reaching consequences. I firmly believe that our son would be dead right now if our marriage had not been restored. Our marriage surely would not have been restored if Lou had not held fast to Jesus and decided to remain a faithful covenant keeper instead of abandoning her marriage vows and "getting on with her life" as many advised her to do. Our son's very life was at stake, but God totally turned things around as I brought my life and our marriage back in line with God.

LOU: Your faith is a powerful witness both to your spouse and to others. When your spouse does come home, a whole new battle begins. Satan doesn't give up. If you have been apart for a long time as Tom and I were, you may have grown accustomed to an independent lifestyle again. There is a lot of dying to self and independence that has to be given up. It was not easy for either of us when Tom first returned, but we have both learned more and more how to die to self and let Jesus Christ in us live. Tom and I have been back together now just a little over seven years and I praise the Lord for not only the end result, but also for the journey. I can honestly say now that He gives you above and beyond anything you have ever dreamed or hoped for.

This is a beautiful story of God's healing and restoration. It was not an easy path for Lou to walk, nor was it short, but she would certainly say now that it was worth it. When Tom left and her house built on sand came crashing down, Lou allowed God to sweep away the rubble, expose the faulty foundations of her life and marriage and begin to rebuild her life on a solid foundation. You can see from their description of their early life together that Lou was a weak, reactive, emotionally dependent person, consumed in idolatry toward her husband. Tom, on the other hand, was a reactive, independent person consumed with self-reliance and self-accomplishment and ultimately idolatry toward self.

This marriage, as a result, had no chance of prospering built upon these faulty values and character qualities. Satan meant to use this weak and faulty foundation to destroy their family and lives. God did not lead Tom to leave or enter into adultery. God however, is an opportunist, and He did utilize the occasion of the circumstance to expose the faulty foundation and establish a new strong foundation. During the six years of separation, God totally transformed both Tom's and Lou's lives. He broke the idolatry toward Tom, and grew Lou up emotionally from a state of dependence to one of independence. The Lord grew her spiritually, implanted some of His deeply held values, and taught her how to make proactive choices, independent of peoples' opinions, circumstances, or emotions. At the same time Tom was totally stripped of his pride, self-reliance, and emotional independence.

By the time Tom and Lou were reunited, they had both grown spiritually and emotionally to the point where they were ready to learn how to establish their marriage on an entirely new foundation. They were both ready to let God grow them up into emotional interdependence, where they were free to acknowledge their own weaknesses and needs, primarily concern themselves with the needs of the other and combine their efforts to work together to accomplish God's will and purpose rather than selfishly striving to meet their own needs at the expense of each other.

As Lou mentioned, many times when a spouse comes home there is yet a significant battle to be won. Oftentimes during the separation time, God is growing one or both partners out of a state of emotional dependence into one of independence. When the couple is reunited, God must then grow them together up out of independence into interdependence. This again is a stressful process in which Satan likes to take opportunity to torment one or both spouses with thoughts such as, "You really are irreconcilable," or, "He/she hasn't changed at all and never will," and, "We should never have attempted to get back together." This is a critical time to recognize what is happening and rather than giving up, press in closer to God and let Him change and grow you up.

Over the last seven years together Tom and Lou have learned how to die to self, put each other first and make Jesus Christ the center of their marriage. Today, their family is closer together than they have ever been. Their sons have learned the value of God's faithfulness, pictured by their mother's faithfulness in the sight of their father's unfaithfulness. At this point three of the four sons have been brought into intimate relationship with Jesus Christ as they have observed the radical transformation in the lives of their parents. The name and image of Jesus has been upheld in this marriage and family and many have been won to Christ as a result of one woman's choice to believe that God is still a God of miracles instead of believing the opinions of the people around her.

Chapter 6

Conclusion

In conclusion, let me remind you again that the battle for your marriage is not a battle of flesh and blood, but rather it is a battle against spiritual forces of wickedness who have deceived your spouse and sought to deceive you. Satan hates you and hates even more the image of God represented in your marriage. God, on the other hand, loves you and your spouse. It is His desire to heal you, and totally restore your marriage as a testimony to His glory, while it is Satan's desire to destroy your marriage as a testimony to his glory. There is no neutral ground. Your choice is to either submit yourself to God for the healing of your life and marriage, or submit yourself to Satan for the destruction of your life and marriage. "*Submit therefore to God. Resist the devil and he will flee from you*" (James 4:7). Let's now review seven practical steps you can take to begin the process of healing in your life and marriage.

1. Commit yourself to Jesus Christ and to His plan for your life and marriage. Make certain that you are born again and that your entire life belongs to Jesus to do with as He sees fit. Make certain

that you are committed to be a covenant keeper in your marriage regardless of the choices of your spouse.

2. Reassess the foundational values of your life and commit yourself to allow God to rebuild His values into your life in the areas in which they have not been. You may review the following areas and ask God to change what He needs to:
- Jesus as Lord vs. Idolatry
- Proactivity vs. reactivity
- Emotional interdependence vs. dependence or independence
- God's Word as absolute vs. God's Word as relative to be proven by experience
- Self-sacrifice vs. self gratification and selfishness
- Covenant in marriage vs. contract in marriage

3. Relinquish your marriage partner to God. Relinquish your right to have a marriage partner and renounce your ability to change your spouse.

4. Learn to pray daily <u>for</u> your marriage and <u>against</u> the deceptive strongholds of the enemy in your own and in your spouse's lives.

5. Seek the Lord to get a revelation of God's view and plan for the restoration of your marriage. Begin to exercise faith in God's power and ability to restore rather than in Satan's ability to destoy or in the mere circumstances at hand.

6. If you are already separated from your spouse, call Covenant Keepers and either start or get involved in a support group in your local area. (918) 743-0365. If you are not yet separated and your spouse may be willing to participate with you in a marriage group, call *Marriage Ministries International*[1] (303) 730-3333.

7. Take part in a *Family Foundations Basic Seminar*. This seminar will help identify from the Word of God more root causes of personal and marital dysfunction and bring about much healing to your life. (303) 797-1139.

Take great courage in the fact that it is the Lord Himself Who will rebuild the wall of your life and marriage on a sure, strong foundation. Satan will send many circumstances and people to discourage you just as he did to Nehemiah as the wall around ancient Jerusalem was rebuilt. I believe that the Lord would say to you today these same words that Nehemiah spoke to those rebuilding the wall in his day:

> *"Do not be afraid of them; remember the Lord who is great and awesome, and fight for your brothers, your sons, your daughters, your wives, and your houses"* (Nehemiah 4:14b).

Let's agree together in prayer right now for the restoration of your life and marriage:

Heavenly Father, I thank You that You love me. Thank You for exposing faulty foundations in my life and for establishing your character and values within me. I believe that You are a God of miracles Who can heal marriages and even resurrect those that are dead. Father, thank You for sending Jesus Christ to die for my selfishness and sin. Lord Jesus, I commit my life and my marriage to You. Forgive me for my sin and foolishness. Lord, do what ever You need to do in my life to make me the kind of person You want me to be. This day, I let go of my spouse to You. I believe that You alone have power to change him/her, so I relinquish that job to You. I set myself in agreement with You this day for the healing and restoration of my marriage. I set myself against Satan and all powers of darkness and I command you in the name of the Lord Jesus Christ to terminate your deception of my marriage partner and loose him/her right now. Lord Jesus, I commit myself by Your grace to uphold Your covenant image in my marriage that my family and others might know who You are. Thank You in advance, Lord, for healing our marriage and so changing each of us that we will truly become the man and woman of each others' dreams. I pray these things, Father, with the authority of the name of the Lord Jesus Christ. Amen!

---

[1]*Marriage Ministries, International* P.O. Box 1040 Littleton, Colorado 80160 ph. (303) 730-3333

You won't want to miss the:
Family Foundations Basic Seminar

What Is It?

An intensive time of teaching from God's Word, followed by sharing, prayer, and ministry in small groups. As teaching topics are brought up, the small groups give opportunity for ministry in that specific area of the individual's life, marriage, or family. The seminar is conducted in a Thursday evening, Friday evening, and all day Saturday format.

Topics include:

Communication

Recognizing different levels of communication.
Resolving Conflicts.

Purpose and Plan

Overview of God's plans and purposes for the individual and family.

Identity and Destiny

7 Critical Times of Blessing.

Life Patterns

8 Adult Life Patterns.
Impact of lack of blessing or the cursing of identity.

Curses and Blessing

Releasing God's Blessing.
Practical steps to freedom from cursing.
Personal Ministry.

Vision Of Family Foundations

It is our vision and purpose to help reimpart back into the culture of the body of Christ, those safeguards which facilitate the natural impartation to people of identity and destiny from God, without such, the devil has been allowed to impart his message of worthlessness and purposelessness to millions of people throughout the earth.

Who should come?

Anyone desirous of lasting change in your life. Many times we see unpleasant, or unhealthy patterns in our lives, but don't know why they are there and/or can't seem to change. This ministry is designed to identify root causes and bring lasting change to these areas.

For a schedule of future seminars or for information on how your church can schedule a *Family Foundations Basic Seminar*, please mail the attached form or call,

(303) 797-1139

Please send me information about the seminars.

Name ______________________

Address ______________________

City, State, Zip ______________________

Telephone ______________________

Mail to:

Family Foundations
P.O. Box 320
Littleton, Colorado 80160
(303) 797-1139

Family Foundations
P.O. Box 452
Corinda, Queensland 4075
Australia

Family Foundations
P.O. Box 52
Rugeley, Staffs.
WS15 3YZ
England